International Institute for Labour Studies

NEW APPROACHES TO POVERTY ANALYSIS AND POLICY – II

Reducing poverty through labour market policies

Edited by José B. Figueiredo
and Zafar Shaheed

A CONTRIBUTION TO THE WORLD SUMMIT FOR SOCIAL DEVELOPMENT

339.46
N532
VOL. 2

ISBN 92-9014-535-8

First published 1995

Copies can be ordered directly from: ILO Publications, International Labour Office, CH-1211 Geneva 22 (Switzerland).

Preface

Fifty years ago the ILO adopted its Declaration of Philadelphia which was to serve as its postwar charter. The Declaration affirmed that poverty anywhere constitutes a danger to prosperity everywhere; that labour is not a commodity; and that freedom of expression and of association are essential to sustained progress. The task for the international community was to carry on the "war against want", both within nations and by concerted international effort.

The fight against poverty and for social justice lies at the heart of all the ILO's concerns. It runs through the ILO's work in such areas as employment, social security, minimum legal provisions for the conditions of work and for relationships within the world of work; and in the broader governance of civil society itself.

The attempt to integrate normative social policies with macro-economic strategies and with institutional change is the essential hallmark of ILO action against poverty. The ILO's approach has three characteristics. First, poverty is not viewed as merely residual or incidental, but as related to the structure and functioning of economic and social institutions. Poverty cannot be understood solely in terms of jobs, but in terms of the social context in which such jobs are embedded. Secondly, the poor have always been viewed as potential social actors rather than as targets for policy. The emphasis on the organization of social actors and their participation in development reflects the tripartite dynamic of the ILO. Thirdly, domestic anti-poverty action has always been set within the external environment. The ILO's concern in the 1950s and 1960s with growth and balance of payments constraints, and in the 1980s with economic stabilization and structural adjustment, are examples of this perspective. It is challenged by the process of globalization at the beginning of the new millenium.

In the last 50 years, per capita income has tripled, but income disparities have doubled. Seven hundred and fifty million people in developing countries are either unemployed or under-employed, a good proportion of them living in conditions of absolute poverty. In the developed economies, 35 million people are unemployed, and the share of precarious, low-quality jobs is continuing to grow. Growth has not led to the automatic eradication of poverty; neither is poverty afflicting solely those without work. The social dilemmas of transition in Eastern and Central Europe, and the problems of Africa, have all served to bring the issue of poverty to the forefront of global agendas.

On the occasion of the 50th anniversary of the Declaration of Philadelphia, the International Institute for Labour Studies reviewed the ILO's experience in this field, to identify options for future strategies. The symposium on "Poverty: New approaches to analysis and policy", organized by the Institute on 22-24 November 1993, brought contributions from a broad spectrum of opinion, including academic researchers, ILO staff, members of the ILO's constituencies and those concerned with the formulation of anti-poverty policies. The intention was to explore innovations, both in the analysis of the problem and in the design of policy, and to bring researchers together with practitioners in identifying promising avenues for future ILO work.

The symposium reviewed past and current ILO research and policy approaches to poverty, and examined recent trends and new options which have emerged in the theoretical and empirical literature. It analysed different aspects of anti-poverty policies: macro-economic and sectoral policies; labour market policies; policies to promote social coherence including social security and other forms of social protection; and the organization and representation of the poor.

The main contributions to this symposium are being published in three monographs. Monograph I comprises a critical review of ILO's action against poverty, including a broad analysis of research issues, a bibliography of ILO publications, and a summary of discussions in the symposium. Monograph II includes papers on the relationship between labour market policies and poverty. It evaluates in particular the potential impact of minimum wages, training, and labour market regulation on the incidence of poverty. Monograph III examines macro-economic and structural adjustment policies in terms of their contribution to poverty eradication in different parts of the world.

Many at the ILO and at the Institute have contributed to this work. Their names appear in each monograph, and their contribution is gratefully acknowledged. I would, however, like to make particular mention of my former colleague, Mr. Gerry Rodgers, whose vision and commitment made the symposium possible.

January 1995   Padmanabha Gopinath
                                          Director of the International Institute
                                                      for Labour Studies

Contents

Acknowledgements

Many people were involved in the production of this monograph. First, we should like to thank the authors, who were extremely cooperative in reworking the papers they wrote for the Poverty Symposium in a more appropriate form following the discussions at the meeting. We should also like to thank participants in the Symposium who, either in public or in private, commented upon the contributions.

We have been greatly assisted in the preparation of this monograph by a number of colleagues and friends, in particular: Gerry Rodgers and Ajit Bhalla, who provided many useful comments and editorial advice; Carmen Ruppert, who retyped and corrected most of the contributions; Hazel Cecconi, who copy edited, formatted and proof-read the papers and did the graphic work. This joint effort has resulted in a volume which we hope contains useful material for those concerned with the ways in which poverty can be alleviated.

J68
I38

Introduction:
Reducing poverty through
labour market policies

edd.

Research on poverty and labour markets has tended to follow rather independent routes, concentrating on the analytical concerns of each of these two subject areas without sufficiently exploring their inter-relationships. Studies on poverty have mainly addressed issues related to the measurement, identification and characteristics of the poor. Labour markets have been mainly analysed either as a means to promote develop-ment; as a resource allocation mechanism; or as a social institution. And although some of the more obvious interrelationships — such as the effects of living conditions on labour productivity or of subsistence wages or labour market segmentation on poverty — have been explored, they have not been a priority, as the literature indicates in these respective fields of analysis. Similarly, but with a focus on structural adjustment processes, the World Bank has also detected such a gap in the literature. It has recently published two volumes containing papers presented at a series of con-ferences on the role of labour markets in the transmission of effects of adjustment processes on the poor.[1] As could be expected, the lack of an integrated view to orient research and the development of two different schools of study — one focusing on poverty and the other on labour markets — have together resulted in different approaches and policy pre-scriptions. Actions taken to alleviate poverty have therefore proved to be unsatisfactory, either by failing to reduce the incidence of poverty or by not reaching the neediest of the poor. In one way or another, this argument cuts across all the chapters in this monograph. These chapters provide suggestions on how labour market policies might be more effectively deployed in addressing poverty. Therefore, while referring in some cases to the role of the ILO, they help to clarify certain ambiguities in these two

---

[1] S. Horton et al.: *Labour markets in an era of adjustment* (Washington, DC, World Bank, EDI Development Studies, May 1994).

areas, and to correct for some analytical biases. The policy issues raised address a variety of themes, such as labour market regulations, social security, education and training and labour-management relations, and in so doing present a number of heuristically useful taxonomies pertaining to poverty and its determinants.

I.   Policies and the labour-poverty nexus

A major social policy concern is the precise identification of the target groups, e.g. the poor. This question is raised by many authors in this monograph and, with reference to developing countries, it is recalled for instance that poverty and unemployment are not necessarily congruent; the poor are often employed irregularly at low wages, or derive low incomes from self-employment based on low assets (Chapter 4). Elsewhere, a series of conditions for determining which are the poor households is proposed. These are: a high rate of unemployment and/or dependency; employment in low-skilled jobs and/or low skill endowment; weak bargaining power; and realization of only a small proportion of the potential skill/qualification or productivity in the job (Chapter 2). It is also proposed that focusing on child labourers, women and the disabled is insufficient and that it is necessary to define subgroups within each vulnerable group and to distinguish between them in order to devise effective policies (Chapter 3). These approaches help to overcome any misconception regarding unidirectional causation of poverty and labour market characteristics.

On the matter of policy instruments, and within a broad social security perspective, there is an attempt to place them in three categories: *promotional* (improvement of endowments, exchange entitlements, real incomes and social consumption); *preventive* (measures to avert deprivation in specific ways); and *protective* (or safety net measures, to provide relief from deprivation). All three types are necessary, but the burden on safety nets should be decreased and their role regarded as a sort of last resort. This holistic approach flies in the face of much of the current emphasis on safety-net approaches to social security (Chapter 4). Social security mechanisms are also capable of becoming more operational as active labour market policies. Actually, unemployment insurance can raise the reservation wage of workers, an important condition for breaking the vicious circle of low-valued human capital chasing low-value jobs. The reduction in labour supply should increase the bargaining power of all workers. However, this can work only if the insurance scheme stops paying benefits when the worker finds a job; in practice, it seems that workers can continue to receive unemployment benefits from having lost a formal sector job, while unofficially taking informal sector or part-time jobs. This situation can perpetuate and expand the informalization and the precariousness of the labour market. The suggested active labour market approach would require further administrative and technical finesse in devising and applying social security schemes (Chapter 2).

Related to the above, there are some suggestions on ways of partly recouping the social costs of abusive termination of employment by employers, proposing that firms that lay off workers too frequently should be financially penalized. The money obtained from imposing such penalties, however, should not be given to individual workers — who might then conceivably be tempted to seek such terminations — but rather should be invested in unemployment insurance programmes, pension funds and other collective labour market programmes. With reference to ways of increasing labour effort and thereby productivity, it is argued that lengthening employment contracts and providing training will help to improve the flow of information and of cooperation between employers and workers (Chapter 2).

The question of the deficiency of general education determining a "precarious" entry into the labour market and perpetuating a vicious circle of low skill endowment is also raised many times (Chapters 2, 3 and 4). Among others, it is proposed that the opportunity cost of staying at school be reduced by the state paying a fixed amount per family (or mother) to keep its young members in the school system, thereby increasing the demand for schooling by the poor. Programmes which are aimed at improving the quality of the labour force are also recommended. They include measures such as incentives for on-the-job training and retraining for the unemployed and credits for the improvement of the general educational level of the youth. Another highlighted point is that to have a significant effect on poverty, educational and training programmes should be based on a detailed identification of the labour market position of the most needy (Chapter 1). More specifically, it is proposed that as far as women are concerned, such initiatives should aim at increasing their productivity in both domestic and professional work (Chapter 6).

As a major source of employment and income of the poor, the small and micro-firms in the informal sector are focused upon in most of the chapters and, among other issues, the need to improve labour market information available to such firms is considered. These enterprises tend to select employees on the basis of informal contacts and information, resulting in high rates of turnover, low productivity and low wages. It is also suggested that there should be considerable scope for extending coverage of labour market regulations to this sector in those developing countries in which considerable economic growth and industrialization have occurred. It is also proposed that public employment services should collaborate closely with training institutions to provide appropriate occupational information, as well as providing counselling on training and retraining for the workforce and enterprises in the informal sector (Chapter 2). There are arguments countering the traditional view that at least one regulatory mechanism, the minimum wage, necessarily increases inequalities between the formal and informal sector. The reason for this is that, where low-income families are major buyers of the relatively cheaper consumption goods and services typically produced by the informal sector, a reduction in the minimum wage could reduce demand for these products, thereby reducing employment and earnings in the sector (Chapter 5).

The much debated question of publicly sponsored employment schemes is discussed in some of the chapters. While conceding that these schemes certainly deserve a place in poverty alleviation programmes, it is argued that they should meet a number of conditions if they are to provide long-term solutions. In particular, such schemes should produce durable products and assets, thereby providing wider indirect benefits to the region in question. The need for these initiatives to be accompanied by meaningful on-the-job training programmes is particularly emphasized. Wider indirect benefits would be forthcoming from special employment programmes if wages in these programmes had the effect of raising the market wage rate by providing a bargaining counter for other rural workers. However, this would conflict with the objective of maximizing employment, which in turn leads to the conclusion that minimum wages, if enforced, would offer greater potential for transfers than employment schemes which pay less than the minimum wage. The vexed area of application and enforcement of minimum wages in rural areas suggests the introduction of measures, such as improved information on rates and penalties for violation; special enforcement emphasis for time-bound activities, in which both bargaining strength of labour is relatively strong and wages earned amount to a sizeable proportion of annual wage incomes; and local wage-monitoring committees with representation from both male and female agricultural workers (Chapters 2 and 4).

Minimum wage-fixing and its relationship to poverty is discussed in greater depth. It is especially emphasized that one should go beyond uni-directional and limited approaches to tackling poverty, and minimum wage policy needs to be combined with redistributive transfer programmes and a realignment of macro-economic and social policy stressing redistribution, equity and solidarity. To do this it is necessary to address the characteristics of those workers earning the minimum wage, in order to identify its role as an element of total household income and as an instrument of social transfer policies better adapted to a targeting approach. This requires detailed information on the pattern of distribution of wages and earnings. Improving the effectiveness of minimum wages will require strengthening the representation of employers and workers on the minimum wage-fixing bodies, improving their capacity to collect and analyse data, and above all in enhancing the enforcement capacity of the competent authorities. Aside from such important issues, if minimum wage fixing is to be really relevant to broader sections of the poor, there is the need to ensure organization and representation of the poor so that, inter alia, they have a meaningful voice vis-à-vis institutions concerned with minimum wage-fixing (Chapter 5).

The labour market-poverty nexus is also treated from a more general perspective. It is argued that the corresponding interrelationships should be more fully acknowledged and evidence is provided on how labour market vulnerability is associated with deprivation. This is done on the basis of data drawn from surveys of households in selected urban areas in three continents — Asia, Africa and Latin America. In such contexts, unemployment — which for some time has been treated as a phenomenon affecting mostly the "rich" and the workers in the formal sector — also appears to be increasingly associated with low productivity jobs and the more destitute household groups. The latter have the highest unemployment and dependency rates, mainly as a result of the more difficult access to (and the more limited) job opportunities which are open to them. Labour market segmentation severely limits upward mobility. It appears that workers in the lowest labour strata tend to be trapped in irregular, insecure and low-paid jobs without any prospects of career improvement. Holding such jobs also proves to be closely linked to situations of deprivation. The more vulnerable workers — such as marginal self-employed and unprotected irregular wage earners — are mainly found to be heads (or secondary members) of destitute households. Moreover, it is in this group of households headed by such workers, where the incidence of poverty is the highest, that the relatively largest proportion of poor families is found (Chapter 1).

II. The poor groups: their characteristics and heterogeneity

The analytical basis for the above policy recommendations constitutes the other major contribution of this monograph. One major focus is on the characterization of the vulnerable groups. Such groups are usually defined and identified based on observable physical characteristics, such as age (children, youth, the elderly), sex (women), ethnicity/race (minority groups), or physical disability (disabled). There are, of course, some important vulnerable groups which are not so easily recognizable, such as the long-term unemployed, migrants, and some religious groups. However, all vulnerable groups have one thing in common. That is, they are disadvantaged or handicapped in the labour market, either because of:

(i) their characteristics (such as limited education, skill or experience; constraints on behaviour due to household responsibilities or cultural mores);

(ii) functioning of the labour market and processes of exclusion from the labour market (such as discriminatory practices related to employment opportunities, lack of access to credit markets and to technology);

(iii) macro-economic and labour market conditions (such as structural adjustment programmes; globalization of production; transition to a market economy; economic recession).

This implies that appropriate policy prescriptions for vulnerable groups will depend very much on macro-economic conditions, stage of development and the particular vulnerable group concerned (Chapter 3).

Another important feature is heterogeneity among vulnerable groups — child workers, women and the disabled — in terms of their labour market disadvantage and poverty. In the former, this is determined through the differentiation which labour market segmentation implies even among workers in the lowest productivity and income jobs. In the latter, the differentiation is illustrated by distinguishing between the assistance required by the permanent (or long-term) poor, the transient poor and the new-poor, respectively, or by indicating the different sets of unsatisfied needs faced by deprived households, even if they live in the same geographical area. The need for more analytical work to understand better the causes of the heterogeneity of vulnerable situations is also stressed. The generation of adequate statistical data should be both more specific — for instance, gender-specific — and also integrated, in the sense of combining information on labour and living conditions of vulnerable groups. This should facilitate the development of appropriate indicators to monitor the situation of such groups, especially during economic and political changes and transitions, and to enhance the process of evaluating the effectiveness of policies, programmes and projects (Chapters 1 and 6).

Despite major differences between various vulnerable groups, interestingly enough there are a number of common features as regards appropriate policies and research directions. First, there is a need to identify and distinguish between various subgroups within each vulnerable group in order to devise effective policies. Secondly, it is important to emphasize policies which will promote the entry of vulnerable group members into the mainstream labour market; this, in turn, implies a need to de-emphasize isolated projects that tend to be small in size (with little impact) and which also tend to reinforce the present segregated position in the labour market of persons from vulnerable groups. Thirdly, skill acquisition is critical if persons from vulnerable groups are to compete effectively in the labour market. Fourthly, there is a need to assist persons from vulnerable groups by creating labour market and non-labour market facilitating policies, in order to reduce the constraints on labour market participation. Fifthly, there is a need for research into the reasons for labour market disadvantage as seen from the employer's viewpoint, since the role played by the demand for labour in establishing and perpetuating discrimination is very important, albeit not yet well understood (Chapter 3).

Women, as constituting probably the largest among the vulnerable groups, are given special attention in this monograph. A detailed analysis on the basis of wide empirical evidence is made on their living conditions and labour situation. There is an outline of the particular features of poor women and female-headed households which indicates how a process of feminization of poverty is taking place. By contrasting female-headed households with others, an attempt is made to identify some of the specificities of such households, notably by highlighting the more "family-conscious" attitudes of women. Reference is made in particular to the trade-offs faced by women in allocating their time between work, leisure and child care, and to their relatively large involvement in community associations so as to compensate for the loss of family services previously provided by the state (Chapter 6).

III. Organization of the monograph

As a whole, this monograph has been designed as a balanced number of chapters having a more general and a more specific perspective on the analytical and policy issues bearing on the interrelationship between poverty and labour markets. The first two chapters address respectively the broad analytical (Chapter 1) and policy (Chapter 2) aspects of this inter-relationship, raising important matters, such as the need to define analytical categories which apply to both the study of labour markets and poverty; identifying the commonalities in the way this interrelationship operates in different economic and social contexts; offering an assessment of the effectiveness of the current employment policies for alleviating poverty; determining what adjustments or reinterpretations, notably on the notion of labour flexibility and protection, would be required in order to reflect better the changing economic environment; considering how adequately such policies do reflect the demands from the poorest groups, e.g. are the jobs being created and the training programmes adequate. Chapter 3 attempts to treat jointly such analytical and policy concerns. It does so by overviewing and comparing the structure of needs and that of the cor-rective actions, i.e. by identifying the main vulnerable groups and their characteristics and the way labour market policies have managed to faci-litate the access of members of these groups to the labour market, to "good" jobs and education. Chapter 4, the first in the series of more specific chapters, focuses on social security. On the basis of similar analysis presented in the second part of a well-known book on social security in developing countries,[2] it highlights the most relevant characteristics of some representative countries for the design of an appropriate social security system and concludes with a series of very precise recommendations for action. Chapter 5 provides an in-depth review of the role of minimum wage policies in the context of more general redistributive programmes. It addresses the currently debated issue of the social and economic effects of minimum wages and attempts to identify the major gaps in national wage and related policies, which should be filled so as to produce more positive effects on poverty. Chapter 6 deals with the situation of women, as one of the increasingly large and vulnerable groups in the context of low-income countries. This chapter reviews empirical evidence on the relatively worse and worsening position of women (and

---

[2] E. Ahmad et al.: *Social security in developing countries* (Oxford, Clarendon Press, 1991).

children) relative to men, and concludes by identifying the implications for the design of a research and policy agenda for the group of women.

All the chapters of this monograph seem to confirm that focusing on the interrelationships between labour market characteristics and institutions and poverty is not only analytically necessary, but would also help to fight poverty in a more efficient manner. They converge in arguing for more decentralized and participatory institutional arrangements with regard to design and application of labour market policies addressing poverty. At the same time they are concerned that labour market regulations be prevented from degenerating into mere dogma, in the absence of reliable information on their socio-economic effects. These chapters also identify the need for research to ascertain the effects of labour standards and labour market regulations on growth, employment and productivity. An integrated approach to poverty and labour market analysis will contribute to such policy research.

José B. Figueiredo
International Institute
for Labour Studies
International Labour Office

Zafar Shaheed
Labour Law and
Labour Relations Branch
International Labour Office

1 Poverty and labour markets in developing countries

José B. Figueiredo, Jean-Pierre Lachaud
and Gerry Rodgers[1]

LDC's

O15

J2Q

I32

J64

I. Introduction

The literature on both poverty and labour markets is substantial, that on the interrelationships between the two distinctly less so. Of course, much research on poverty looks at employment patterns and their effects on income and living standards, but the sources of these employment patterns in labour market mechanisms are addressed more rarely. Nor has much labour market analysis examined the effects of precarious living conditions on employment and labour productivity. The reasons are to a large extent historical. The labour market, in low-income settings at least, has mainly been regarded as a means to promote development. Most attention has been paid to formal labour market structures and institutions and their effects on the efficiency of resource allocation. In developing this perspective, analysts have faced a series of challenges as the limitations of traditional market-based theories in explaining wage and employment structure and dynamics have become more apparent. While some of the responses to these challenges — subsistence or efficiency wage models, for instance — are directly related to poverty in obvious ways, this theme has not been a priority in the literature. At the same time, poverty analysis has been dominated by studies of the identification of the poor and their characteristics. The measurement of poverty has become more sophisticated, with a shift from simple poverty lines to more multifaceted and multidisciplinary frameworks which could better deal with the variety of situations and dimensions of poor communities. But policy to reduce poverty has remained concentrated on rather direct intervention to raise incomes or provide goods and services to the poor: in so far as the labour

---

[1] International Institute for Labour Studies.

market is involved, it is mainly as an instrument supporting employment creation programmes.

And yet a strong case can be made not only that poverty does affect the way labour markets operate, but — more important — that policy initiatives to reduce or eliminate poverty are likely to be much more effective if they are rooted in analysis of how labour markets produce or reproduce poverty. For this purpose, it is important not to take too narrow a definition of the term labour market: informal employment, self-employment and even family work should be taken into account, if only because these different types of labour usually occur in situations where there is also wage work, so that self-employment in the informal sector, say, will interact with or depend on wage labour because of indirect supply or demand relationships. But even if we restrict the term to wage labour, it is clear that the labour market is an important transmission mechanism which links overall economic performance to poverty. For instance, it is widely recognized that the effects on the poor of economic restructuring and stabilization programmes have to a large extent been channelled through the labour market. More generally, employment levels, which have been described as the "iron" link between economic development and poverty, should be seen not as a simple product of macro-economic mechanisms but as an outcome of both aggregate factors and the labour market mechanisms which covert these into jobs and distribute them among different population groups.

This short Chapter reflects on how such issues might be addressed, taking into account recent work at the International Institute for Labour Studies. First we very briefly consider some relevant aspects of labour market structure, and of poverty, before considering some of the ways in which they interact, and the evidence on these interactions. The focus is implicitly or explicitly on urban labour markets.

II. Relevant features of the labour market

Many aspects of labour market analysis have a direct or indirect bearing on poverty, but there are a number of topics which are of particular importance, especially those concerned with inequalities in access to jobs, with the stratification of jobs, and with the factors which generate particular labour market features and mechanisms at low income levels.

Unemployment and underemployment: A major feature of industrialization in most countries — the main exceptions being East Asia — has been that even during periods of economic expansion, insufficient jobs have been created to absorb the increase in labour supply resulting from migration and population growth. Since it was generally assumed that the poor could not survive unemployment, excess labour supply was thought to manifest itself above all in underemployment in the informal sector. The empirical evidence does not support this model, and open unemployment has been rising rapidly in some parts of the world (e.g. urban Africa) and is probably becoming a widespread source of extreme poverty. What is more, there are signs that employment elasticities are declining, so that economic growth generates even fewer jobs, in developing and industrialized countries alike. There are mechanisms at work here which are not well understood — the creation of jobs involves social and institutional relationships, and not just economic and technological ones, and it is urgent to understand these processes better. In any case, it seems that the volume of employment is bound up with the types of jobs that are being created, and who gets them, so that there is a complex relationship between the growth of employment and of unemployment. Underemployment, in its various forms, also arises out of these relationships. Unemployment and underemployment, then, are not just the result of excess labour supply, but rather reflect important mechanisms linking labour markets and poverty.

Wage determination in low-income settings: Even market models of wage determination have to recognize that there is a floor to the price of labour because of the need for subsistence. Early models of dualistic development took subsistence in the rural sector as the reference point (so that wages remained constant close to subsistence level until excess labour supply was exhausted). Efficiency wage models subsequently explored the relationship between wages and productivity. In low-income settings the basic assumption is that there is a physical relationship between food intake and work capacity. It can be shown that in such circumstances there is a wage below which it is not in the employer's interest to reduce wages further, because efficiency losses outweigh cost reductions. So various economic mechanisms may lead to a floor below which wages will not fall. But wage-fixing also depends on a series of institutional factors which may also generate a floor to wages: for instance, there may be a powerful social notion of what constitutes a "fair" wage, leading to resistance if attempts are made to lower the wage beyond this point (see for instance Solow, [1990]). On the other hand, the relative power of different groups in the labour market will also lead to wage differentials, so that the level of the wage floor will not be the same for all groups. The existence of a wage floor may lead to growth in parallel, marginal self-employment at lower income levels if it restricts demand for labour.

There are a number of other specific factors involved in wage-setting at low income levels. On the whole, the working poor are less well organized than others and this undermines their attempts to gain improved wages and working conditions. Irregular and casual employment also affects the way wages are set and paid. Discrimination may be important in creating groups of workers who are particularly vulnerable to low wages.

Heterogeneity: Industrialization is accompanied by a process of "heterogenization" of the labour market which goes far beyond the dualistic model. This process implies that there develop not one or two but several markets or segments of the labour market which are characterized by differences in type of jobs, rules of access and remuneration. The development of research along these lines has suggested that a distinction between "horizontal" and "vertical" segmentation is needed in order to obtain reasonably homogeneous analytical categories — vertical segmentation referring to different types of labour market contributing to a single process of production, horizontal to distinct processes of production and labour use co-existing within the same economy.

A variety of theoretical models exist which try to explain heterogeneity in the labour market. The human capital model attributes wage disparities to productivity differentials between workers, not to segmentation. Models of discrimination interpret labour market heterogeneity in terms of the way societies offer different life chances to different groups among their members. More structural models treat segmentation as essentially determined by technology, or designed to weaken solidarity among different groups of workers. Finally there are two opposed views, one proposing that segmentation is the result of the malfunctioning of the market and that it would disappear provided corrective policies were applied. The other states that segmentation is the result of the confrontation of social actors, in society in general and in the labour market in particular, who have very distinct objectives and conflicting interests as well as very different organization and representation, and negotiating capabilities and power.

The importance of these issues for poverty lies in the tendency of labour market heterogeneity to give rise to strata of low-paid, poorly-protected, irregular jobs. Segmentation as a concept is particularly relevant because it implies that there is relatively little mobility between different parts of the labour market, so that the poor become trapped in these low-income segments. So understanding the processes underlying stratification is important for understanding the sources of poverty. Some of the key elements are regularity, protection and autonomy of jobs, and a series of studies has been carried out which tries to capture the structuring of the labour market into different types of jobs in terms of factors such as these.

The institutional framework: Labour market institutions are diverse, and include not only the formal instruments such as collective bargaining systems and labour legislation but also a range of informal institutions and socially determined patterns of behaviour. While the formal labour market institutions relevant for poverty may be more visible (e.g. minimum wage legislation), many informal institutions also have a major impact on the poor, among other reasons because they affect all three topics discussed above (unemployment, wages and heterogeneity). A particularly important issue concerns the institutions for access to the labour market. While formal institutions involving schooling and training, competition and other codified selection procedures may be important in some parts of the labour market, for many jobs particularistic mechanisms such as inter-personal networks and contacts will dominate. These informal institutions may in turn reflect underlying social rules about the rights of different members of the society, the hierarchy of status and opportunity, the transmission of welfare within kin and community networks, and the like.

III. Poverty

There are also a number of aspects of poverty which are of particular relevance to analysing the relationship with the labour market.

Complexity: There are both simple and complex notions of poverty. The simplest, involving falling below a subsistence threshold, is most appealing and most widespread. But there are good reasons for trying to go further. There is considerable diversity in needs, and in the means by which they are met, and they generate a complex pattern of inequalities in deprivations and satisfactions. This results not only from the inter-relationships between different demographic, cultural and economic characteristics, but also from the different ways families establish their priorities, and from the patterns of discrimination, inclusion or exclusion to which they are subject. As Streeten [1990] points out, "unfortunately" it is likely that the use of even a priori strongly correlated indicators, such as income, calorie intake and percentage expenditure on food, will identify different population groups as poor. Even in "ultra-poverty" situations, where nutritional inadequacy is widespread, the link between income and nutrition is only strong in some areas — like South and South-East Asia — but not in others — such as Africa. One explanation lies in differences in the social environment of different groups; differences in culture, in access to education and to information systems, in health conditions and access to other social services. But this pattern is also closely bound up with the heterogeneity of production systems, notably in the informal sector, where many of the poor derive a large proportion of their earnings. Thus complexity in the labour market and complexity in the pattern of poverty are interrelated.[2]

Rights, entitlements and deprivation: Poverty is often considered in an absolute sense; those falling below a specified standard are poor. But a persistent theme in the poverty literature relates poverty directly to social rather than absolute standards. Societal institutions or the State define a set of rights and entitlements, and particularly in so far as these involve command over consumption goods the poor are identified as those who are unable to exercise these rights. There is an important link with labour market issues here in that employment may itself belong to the set of rights, and provide both social legitimacy and income. Deprivation concerns not only food and clothing but also deprivation of a social position provided by work. There may also be specific deprivations associated with work, in terms of security (duration of work, safety nets in the absence of employment) and in terms of the quality of employment. Entitlements, in the sense developed by Sen [1981], also involve labour market mechanisms, for the value of entitlements depends on a process of exchange which may be modified over time (catastrophically in the case of famines).

Income sharing arrangements: The ways in which income from work is shared are crucial for determining poverty. In most societies, households of one sort or another provide the basic income-sharing unit. Since households vary greatly in their income-earning power, both between different households and over time, this alone implies both differences in incidence of poverty and differences in labour market strategy. But there are also solidarity mechanisms at community level and broader social security systems at a more general level. These different levels involve different

---

[2] Several attempts have been made to address this question of complexity. For example, one could mention the sensitivity and dominance analysis proposed by Ravallion [1992] to test the consistency of patterns of poverty, both on a cross-section and over-time basis.

types of links with the labour market, particularly in so far as labour market obligations and income entitlements are linked.

Dynamics: Dynamic aspects of poverty provide another source of heterogeneity. There are important movements in and out of situations of deprivation, as individuals gain and lose access to the labour market, as households pass through different parts of the life-cycle, as individual fortunes change. In the United States, for example, but also in a number of Latin American countries, it has been observed that a significant proportion of people who moved below the poverty line did so at the time their family structure changed, e.g. when a female-headed household was formed as a result of the break-up of a nuclear family. New economic phenomena may also create new forms of poverty, and new groups among the poor, and these downwardly mobile groups may be quite different from the long-term deprived. So it is important to distinguish between the permanent as opposed to the transient poor, and also between the recent poor and the long-term poor, whose needs, behaviour patterns and economic characteristics are likely to be very different.

Representation: Poverty also stems from the lack of representation of the poor. This is partly explained by the diversity of the poor — in which labour market segmentation plays a role, since different groups among the poor develop different and sometimes competing interests. Looking at the labour market segments where the more deprived are found, it can be seen that they are also marginalized with respect to access to institutions which provide basic information and skill formation. Moreover, the mainstream labour organizations tend to focus on the core group of workers and less on the physically distant out-workers, the unemployed, etc., i.e. situations in which the poor are over-represented. Non-governmental organizations aimed at representing the poor face the problem that not only do they have limited resources but they tend to be managed by the non-poor on behalf of the poor, a situation which is untenable in the long term (see for instance Lewis [1991]). Even the functioning of new and more adequate institutional mechanisms which were created to monitor specific social initiatives have proved not to be a sufficient condition to reach the poor, at least not the more deprived among the poor (see, for instance, Danziger & Weinberg [1986]; Infante [1993]).

IV. The labour market and poverty

Poverty has causes which go far beyond the labour market and, in particular, it depends on the overall levels of production and productivity. And within the labour market, the poor do not constitute an identifiable group: there are greater or lesser degrees of poverty in different labour market categories. But many labour market mechanisms and patterns are closely associated with poverty, and give insights into the pattern and intensity of poverty, and into the factors concentrating poverty among particular groups. At the same time, the labour market is an important economic mechanism through which poverty is reduced. Recent research at the International Institute for Labour Studies and elsewhere has identified a number of specific relationships which seem to merit more careful attention in future research.

It seems important in the first instance to distinguish between poverty within and poverty outside the labour market; in other words, is poverty associated with the nature of employment and the levels of income which it generates, or is it due to exclusion from access to jobs? Exclusion from regular income opportunities may appear as open unemployment, or as marginality in one form or another — including low productivity street activities, crime or beggary. But it may also be hidden, if particular groups do not appear on the labour market because their opportunities are limited — this is often true of women, for example, and of potential migrants. Exclusion from the labour market may be associated with personal characteristics — disability, for instance, or race. The degree to which labour market exclusion is directly linked to poverty depends on the extent to which state or community safety nets or solidarity networks exist, or whether it affects particular members (women, younger workers) of households where there is another income source. But the process of exclusion itself, in so far as it is concentrated on particular groups, is often wider than the labour market alone, so that exclusion from the labour market may be correlated with exclusion from the safety nets. Exclusion also operates within the labour market, with respect to access to the more desirable jobs — this we comment on below.

At the opposite extreme there is a phenomenon of "overemployment": excessive work, because low productivity or low wages imply that very long hours have to be worked to achieve a subsistence income. This is no doubt the most frequent situation of the poor, and among the self-employed it is likely to be associated with inadequate use of human or physical resources — which is often regarded as a form of underemployment in the literature (in a productivity, rather than a time sense); so underemployment and overemployment coincide. Overemployment may also involve labour force participation by groups for which it is undesirable — child labour, for instance, or work while unfit — with subsequent consequences for personal development or health.

A more classic case concerns the abuse of the position of particular groups of workers, who are vulnerable to manipulation or exploitation. Bonded labour is an obvious example, but the position of temporary migrants may be little better (see, for instance Bremen [1985]). More generally, low skilled and unorganized workers may be unable to obtain decent working conditions and remunerations from employers in the absence of social legislation or in the absence of its effective enforcement.

But the more general issue, which emerges from the preceding sections, concerns the heterogeneity of both poverty and labour markets. How does differentiation in the labour market affect the overall level of poverty and its incidence?

All labour markets exhibit inequality, of course. Productivity differences between occupations, or between individuals with different skill or educational levels, lead to differences in returns to labour which may be regarded as efficient in conventional economic models. This is not true, however, of differences in rewards to individuals with similar abilities and qualifications, as a result of discrimination; nor is it true of differences in rewards to labour which arise out of constraints on entry to particular jobs or sectors. These factors may give rise to poverty because of the emergence of labour market segments in which jobs are irregular, insecure and low paid. These characteristics themselves lead to poverty, which then persists because individuals are trapped in these segments. Mobility between different labour market segments is difficult, because of the credentials, contacts, capital or skills required to move up; many groups are excluded from regular, protected jobs. So entry to low-end jobs virtually precludes subsequent career development. Because of the insecure and irregular nature of the work, workers in these segments are also particularly vulnerable to unemployment. Such patterns can be observed in high-income and in low-income economies alike. In industrialized countries they appear in short-term or casual work, in homework and in some types of self-employment — categories of labour which appear to have increased their share of all jobs over the last 10 to 15 years. In developing countries they show up in the casualization of employment relationships, in marginal self-employment and in various types of unprotected wage employment. That rather similar patterns can be observed in low and high-income environments suggests that at least this aspect of poverty has its roots in labour market structure — increasing aggregate production and average incomes would not be sufficient for its elimination.

On the supply side of the labour market, because of their heterogeneity and the lack of representation in and access to social institutions, the poor have very diverse labour strategies, although the latter have as a common feature to be aimed at neutralizing their intrinsic vulnerability. Another common characteristic is that such strategies are dominated by a context of extreme need. This forces unemployed family members to search for and accept poorly-remunerated jobs or to produce low-quality goods or services for sale. It also undermines the ability to invest in the acquisition of qualifications and skills, so reinforcing the inability of the poor to escape from labour market vulnerability.

The ways in which these relationships affect poverty depend on a series of additional factors. First, labour market outcomes (usually) refer to individuals, and the link with poverty depends on the pattern of earning and dependency in the income-sharing unit. Larger households with single earners are more vulnerable to poverty regardless of labour market characteristics. But there is a tendency for the most adverse labour market situations to be faced by first-time entrants, many of them in households with additional income sources. Secondly, relative deprivation may be closely related to labour market patterns: labour market inequality may be a primary element in felt deprivation, as some attain social integration and regular income through the labour market, while others survive in casual, precarious employment. If poverty is defined in relation to what societies regard as decent minima for all their citizens, then the labour market situation is likely to be an important element in the definition of poverty.

V. Some evidence

Some of these patterns have been explored in recent work at the International Institute for Labour Studies, although much remains to be done. On the whole, the relationship between labour market patterns and poverty is not easy to study with existing data, because the surveys which collect information at the household level on welfare and consumption usually have insufficient data on labour market patterns for each household member, while labour force surveys often have rich information on individuals but little on the households to which they belong. Even in Western Europe, where the data base is otherwise extensive, it is difficult to study the relationship between non-standard work and poverty because the main data sources do not permit it. Research in this area therefore has to rely heavily on fresh data collection. With this in mind, there have been studies based on small-scale surveys in India (Coimbatore, see Harriss et al. [1990]), in several African countries (summarized in Lachaud [1993]) and (on a larger scale) in Brazil (São Paulo, see SEADE [1992]). These studies concentrated exclusively on urban areas. Some of the relevant results are presented in Table 1, in a highly summarized form. The table includes results from Cameroun (Yaoundé) and Burkina Faso (Ouagadougou), as two rather different examples among the several cities studied in this sub-region of Africa. The figures for poverty incidence in the three cities (44 per cent for São Paulo, 42 per cent for Coimbatore,[3] 44 per cent for Ouagadougou and 17 per cent for Yaoundé) of course cannot be directly compared with each other; in particular, the poverty threshold in São Paulo was distinctly higher in real terms than in other two cities. This is normal; poverty is defined in relation to the perceptions and needs of each society.

We will comment on four issues: unemployment; segmentation; household structure; and heterogeneity.

Unemployment: There is a strong association between unemployment and poverty in all three studies. The unemployment rate in deprived households is up to double the average rate, and up to three times the rate for the non-poor. While this is contrary to the popular perception of some years ago that unemployment in low-income countries is mainly a middle-class phenomenon, it is consistent with evidence from elsewhere that open unemployment is a substantial source of poverty (see Rodgers [1989]). The ratio between the number of unemployed persons and the number of income earners tends to be larger — up to twice as large — in poor households as in non-poor ones. But even among the poor, unemployment affects different individuals in different ways. It is, for example, far more pronounced for secondary workers than for heads of households (5 to 10 times higher) and also higher among the young and the more educated. These patterns, of course, affect the relationship with poverty. The relatively high level of unemployment among the more educated suggests that the unemployment figures include some extended job search among the relatively well off, but this is swamped in the aggregate figures by the larger proportion of unemployment linked to poverty. Survival in such situations, in the absence of effective systems of unemployment insurance, depends on intra-family or intra-community transfers, on days of work

---

[3] This figure includes some groups considered above the poverty line in the original study, where 27 per cent of households were found to fall below a poverty line similar to the one used in most official poverty estimates in India.

Table 1: Poverty and the labour market: Some evidence

	São Paulo 1990	Coimbatore 1987	Ouagadougou 1992	Yaoundé 1990-91
Unemployment				
Total	9.4	13.1	25.0	29.3
Among the poor	15.5	18.2	31.9	47.5
Poverty incidence (excluding unemployed)	44.3	42.0	44.1	16.6
Poverty incidence in vulnerable labour status groups	68.6	67.0	65.0	35.6
Share of vulnerable labour status groups in total employment	33.9	29.6	51.0	41.9
Share of vulnerable labour status groups among the employed poor	52.4	47.2	75.1	90.0

Notes: **São Paulo**: All variables (except unemployment) refer to households. "Household labour status" is defined on the basis of a combination of the head's and another selected household member's status in the labour market. Unemployment: *Open unemployment*, Labour market volume, Table 20. Poverty threshold: Household monthly income of 2 minimum wages per capita, Income volume, Table 20. Vulnerable labour status groups comprise households where: the head and the other household member have a vulnerable labour status (i.e. being either a dependant or having an irregular and low-income job; the head has a vulnerable labour status and the other member a non-vulnerable one; the head has a non-vulnerable status and the other member a vulnerable one), Labour market volume, Table 20.

Coimbatore: Unemployment: *Open unemployment last year* (Table 50). Poverty threshold: household weekly income of Rs. 60 per adult equivalent (Table 48); to be consistent with the labour status rates, the unemployed have been excluded from the poverty incidence rate. Vulnerable labour status groups are composed of individuals who are in unprotected-regular-short-term or in unprotected-irregular jobs or are independent wage or marginal self-employed workers (Table 48).

Ouagadougou and Yaoundé: Unemployment: *Open unemployment* (Table E). Poverty threshold: household weekly income of FCFA 2222 (Ouagadougou) and FCFA 2880 (Yaoundé) per adult equivalent (Table B); to be consistent with the labour status rates, the unemployed have been excluded from the poverty incidence rate. Vulnerable labour status groups are composed of heads of households who are in unprotected or irregular jobs, or are marginal self-employed workers (Table C).

Sources: **São Paulo**: SEADE [1992], Labour market and income volumes.
        Coimbatore: Harriss et al. [1990].
        Ouagadougou and Yaoundé: Lachaud [1993].

interspersed with days of unemployment, on the sale of assets, on indebtedness, or on unrecorded marginal work. Of course, survival rates are also certainly lower among the unemployed, although this is something on which there is only anecdotal evidence.

Segmentation: In all four studies, attempts were made to understand the pattern of labour market segmentation in terms such as those discussed above. In the Indian city, seven main categories of jobs (categories of "labour status") were identified, taking into account the distinction between wage work and self-employment, the degree of effective protection of workers through the application of labour legislation or union organization, the regularity of work, its duration, and (in the case of the self-employed) the amount of capital used. Mobility between these categories of labour status was low, suggesting that they gave a good approximation to the pattern of labour market segmentation. The Yaoundé study worked with five types of major labour status: protected wage workers, unprotected regular wage workers, irregular wage workers, self-employed with capital and marginal self-employed. The São Paulo study combined similar labour market categories to those in the previously mentioned studies and derived a labour status for the household as a whole, on the basis of the labour market situation of selected household members. It also used an alternative to the poverty line approach, in which the population was classified into four distinct social groups on the basis of a multivariate analysis based on dwelling, education, income and labour status indicators.

Despite the very distinct economic and social contexts, the three studies all suggest that the identification of vulnerable labour status groups contributes powerfully to the analysis of poverty. Poverty rates in these groups are much higher than in the population at large. Detailed analysis in India using different poverty lines shows that the most vulnerable labour status categories (unprotected irregular wage employment, independent wage work and marginal self-employment; to a lesser extent also short-term regular wage work) systematically have the highest poverty incidence. Results for São Paulo, for instance, show that labour status is the single most important factor explaining differences in poverty between households, while education plays a more limited role. The household sample surveys carried out in Yaoundé, Ouagadougou and in other francophone African capital cities also indicate a close relationship between the more precarious labour status of individuals, as defined by irregularity and lack of protection and capital, unemployment and poverty. A large majority of irregular and marginal self-employed, and to a lesser extent non-protected wage-earners, belong to poor households. For the non-protected wage-earner group, almost one in every two workers is from a poor household. An important issue is whether the head of the household has a vulnerable labour market status; poverty is particularly widespread in households headed by irregular and marginal self-employed workers. This evidence is not conclusive, since it is based on small samples — except in the case of São Paulo — but the similarity in patterns in very different urban situations strongly suggests that more attention to labour market segmentation is needed in future research on poverty.

Household position: Much research has been devoted to and has shown the importance of personal characteristics such as age, sex, house- hold type, migrant status, etc., for assessing deprivation and the quality of insertion into the labour market. Results from the studies referred to above confirm the importance of these issues. They show, for instance, that much variation in poverty between households can be traced to dependency, and the vulnerability to poverty of households with a high proportion of women (especially if the head is a woman) is found here, as in many other studies. But it has also been shown that for such components to explain depriva- tion, they need to be evaluated in relation to labour market conditions. The adverse position of female-headed households, for instance, can be traced in part to the way in which women are over-represented in vulnerable labour market segments.

Heterogeneity: As well as exhibiting the same kind of structural relationships between labour and poverty as in the other cases, the São Paulo exercise also documented heterogeneity in ways which merit further attention. When households were classified in relation to the four welfare indicators included in the study — housing, education, income and labour status — it was found that only 11 per cent of the families cumulate deficiencies with respect to all four indicators. Similar results were found in India — i.e. deprivation in one dimension did not necessarily imply deprivation in all. Moreover it was found that income measures alone seem to be quite incomplete as indicators; the São Paulo survey indicated, for instance, that the "richest" families from the least favoured group, in terms of social indicators, had earnings similar to the average of the socially most favoured group. This survey also illustrated how different socio- economic components have varying importance and meanings for the different social groups. For example, education plays a very significant role for the better-off households while for the most deprived it is the labour status which is the predominant component.

VI. Conclusion

There is quite strong evidence here for a widespread structural relationship between labour market status — including unemployment — and poverty. The heterogeneity of both labour market and poverty situations implies that such relationships are not "uniform" but, on the contrary, they have different meanings and patterns according to the various types and levels of labour market vulnerability, of unemployment situation and of household structure. Models of labour market segmentation can make sense of this complexity by distinguishing different types of jobs which both help to explain labour market functioning and have a direct bearing on the extent and incidence of poverty. But this is not the only aspect of the labour market which is relevant, for it is important to understand the labour institutions which include some in regular employment and exclude others, and the strategies of labour market behaviour which they induce among the poor.

These issues are important not only for research, but also for policy. Targeted action against poverty may well be more effective if vulnerable groups can be identified in terms of detailed labour market position. Intervention in the labour market with a view to reducing poverty also needs to take account of these structural features of labour markets. If the aim is to reduce poverty by widening employment opportunities, labour market segmentation and, more generally, the ways in which jobs are created and access to them controlled, will be important determinants of success or failure.

So more attention needs to be paid to labour market heterogeneity and its causes. But this is only a part of the story: a longer list of relationships between labour market functioning and poverty was outlined in Section IV, and suggests some elements for a research agenda. This is not to say that labour market forces are necessarily the primary causes of poverty, nor that labour market intervention is the most effective form of anti-poverty policy. But it does seem likely that there will be fairly high returns to further research in this area.

Bibliographical references

Bremen, J. 1985. *Of peasants, migrants and paupers: Rural labour circulation and capitalist production in West India.* Delhi, Oxford University Press.

Comercio Exterior. 1992. "La lucha contra la pobreza en América Latina", Vol. 42, No. 4, May. Mexico.

Cortazar, R. 1977. *Necesidades básicas y extrema pobreza.* Santiago de Chile, OIT-PREALC.

Danziger, S.; Weinberg, D. (eds.). 1986. *Fighting poverty: What works and what doesn't.* Harvard University Press.

Glewwe, P.; Hall, G. 1992. "Poverty and inequality during unorthodox adjustment: The case of Peru", Washington, DC, World Bank, LSMS Working Paper No. 86.

Harriss, J.; Kannan, K. P.; Rodgers, G. 1990. *Urban labour market structure and job access in India: A study of Coimbatore.* Research Series 92. Geneva, IILS.

Infante, R. (ed.) 1993. *Deuda social. Desafío de la equidad.* Santiago de Chile, OIT/PREALC.

Lachaud, J.-P. 1993. "Poverty and the urban labour market in sub-Saharan Africa: A comparative analysis", Discussion Paper 55. Geneva, IILS (in French).

Lewis, P. 1991. *Social action and the labouring poor.* New Delhi, Vistaar Publications.

Lille, Université des sciences et technologies de. 1992. *Processus d'exclusion et dynamiques d'emploi*, Journée d'études. Lille, Nov.

Ravallion, M. 1992. "Poverty comparisons. A guide to concepts and methods". LSMS Working Paper No. 88.

Rodgers, G. (ed.). 1989. *Urban poverty and the labour market.* Geneva, IILS/ILO.

Rodgers, G.; Rodgers, J. (eds.). 1989. *Precarious jobs in labour market regulation.* Geneva, IILS and Free University of Brussels.

Rodgers, G.; Wilkinson, F. 1991. "Deprivation and the labour market: Research issues and priorities", in *Labour and Society* (Geneva; IILS), Vol. 16, No. 2.

Sawhill, I. 1988. "Poverty in the US: Why is it so persistent?", in *Journal of Economic Literature* (Nashville), Vol. XXVI, Sept.

SEADE. 1992. *Pesquisa de condições de vida na grande S. Paulo: principais resultados.* São Paulo.

Sen, A. K. 1981. *Poverty and famines: An essay on entitlement and deprivation.* Oxford, Clarendon Press.

Solow, R. 1990. *The labour market as a social institution.* London, Blackwell.

Streeten, P. 1990: "Poverty concepts and measurement", in *The Bangladesh Development Studies* (Dhaka), Vol. XVIII, No. 3, Sept.

2   Active labour market policies and poverty alleviation

I32
J68

Ricardo P. de Barros and José Márcio Camargo[1]

I.   Introduction

Poverty has been a persistent phenomenon in both developed and developing countries. Many factors interact to determine poverty levels in a given country. This paper analyses the role of labour markets in this process and discusses how labour market policies can be used to reduce poverty.

For analytical purposes, labour market policies can be divided into four distinct sets of instruments. First, there are those instruments directed at increasing the rate of employment creation, whatever the quality of the employment generated. Second, there are those instruments directed at increasing the quality of the employment and thus the income level of the poor. Third, policies which increase the quality of the labour force should also be considered labour market policies; and fourth, policies which affect the bargaining power of workers and create incentives for them to provide their full potential qualification in the job. Finally, some policies directed at creating a social safety net to help the working population overcome unemployment or other transitory or even structural conditions that make them poor should also be analysed.

Poverty can be a transitory as well as a structural condition. In the first case, a family's poverty is related to some eventual phenomenon: short-term unemployment, temporary illness, etc. Structural poverty, on the other hand, is a long-term condition and is related to structural factors. Although many of the labour market policies that will be analysed in this

---

[1] Instituto de Planejamento Econômico e Social (IPEA), Instituto de Pesquisas (INPES) and Yale University and Department of Economics of the Pontificio Universidade Católica do Rio de Janeiro, respectively.

paper can be used to reduce transitory poverty, the focus will be on structural poverty.

The chapter is structured as follows. First, an analytical framework will be developed to describe and organize the effects of labour market behaviour on poverty levels. Based on this framework, specific labour market policies will be analysed in subsequent sections. Specifically, Section III will analyse labour market policies meant to increase the rate of employment generated by the economy. Section IV will concentrate on policies which could increase the quality of the employment actually generated. In Section V, policies which improve the quality of the labour force of the poor will be analysed. Section VI will study the effects of different institutional and legislative arrangements on the bargaining power of workers and on the amount of work effort effectively provided by the labour force. Finally, Section VII will present some conclusions. Each section will give examples of how these sets of policies are being (or not being) used in different countries of Latin America.

II. Labour market and poverty [2]

This section presents a framework for analysing the relation between labour market behaviour and poverty. The framework is based on a set of identities which will help to understand this relationship. On the other hand, the distribution of physical wealth (the distribution of land owner-ship, for example), while an important determinant of poverty, will not be dealt with here.

Assuming that the family is the relevant unit to analyse poverty, that the income inside the family is equally distributed and that there is a direct relation between income and basic needs satisfaction, per capita family income can be used as an indicator of poverty level.

If direct income transfers are excluded, per-capita income of a given family is the product of two factors: the average income generated by the family's working members and the total number of family members, including those not working. Thus, if y is the per-capita income of a family with n members, it can be written as:

$$y = \Sigma_{i=1,n} \, y_i/n \equiv \Sigma_{i=1,n} \, (y_i/l).(l/m).(m/n)$$

---

[2] This section is based on Barros & Camargo [1993].

where m = number of family members in the labour force and l = the number of family members working.

The above identity can be expressed in terms of the rate of unemployment (u) and the dependency ratio (d) as:

$$y \equiv w(1 - u)/(1 + d)$$

where $w = \Sigma_{i = 1,n} \, y_i/l$ is the family working members' average income.

By this definition, a family may be poor because the average income level of its working members is small, and/or because the proportion of its members in the labour force is small. It may also be poor if the rate of unemployment of its members in the labour force is high. The behaviour of labour markets can affect directly at least two of these three variables: the family's average income and the rate of unemployment of the economically active family members. In some circumstances (see below), it can also affect the dependency ratio. Thus, an analysis of how these variables are determined is an important step in understanding how the behaviour of labour markets affects poverty.

The average income of a family's working members can be low either because the workers' marginal productivity is low or because they have low bargaining power and so are not able to earn their marginal productivity, or both. Let V_i denote the value of the marginal productivity of the i-th family's working members. So, the average marginal productivity can be written as:

$$v \equiv \Sigma_{i = 1,l} \, V_i/l$$

The bargaining power of the working members can be defined as the ratio between the average earnings (w) and the value of the marginal productivity. So:

$$b \equiv w/v \Rightarrow w \equiv b.v$$

Substituting in the above identity for income:

$$y \equiv b.v.(1 - u)/(1 + d)$$

The average income level of a given family is low if the average bargaining power of its working members, b, or the average value of their marginal productivity, v, are small, or both.

The average marginal productivity of the family's working members depends on the average quality of their jobs which, if constant returns to scale are assumed, will depend on the capital/labour ratio of the employing firm, $g(k)$, and on the quality of the labour supplied by the average family's working members (q). Formally:

$$v = g(k).q$$

where k = capital/labour ratio.

Finally, the quality of the average family's working members will depend on their average potential qualification and on the extent to which they effectively supply this potential qualification in the market — in other words, on the amount of effort they invest in the job. Formally, if p denotes the potential quality of the workers, the extent to which this capacity is realized by the workers can be written as:

$$e \equiv q/p \Rightarrow q \equiv e.p \quad [0 \leq p \leq 1]$$

Thus, substituting these relations in the income equation will give:

$$y = [(1 - u)/(1 + d)].[b.g(k)].[e.p]$$

Based on the above equation, it can be said that a family is poor either because the unemployment rate of its members is high and/or because it has a high dependency ratio. If the unemployment rate of the family's labour force and the dependency ratio are low, the family may still be poor if its members are working in low-quality jobs. Even if the family members are in high-quality jobs, the family may be poor if the bargaining power of its members is so low that they do not earn their marginal productivity. Even if they have high-quality jobs and high bargaining power, they may still be poor if the quality of their labour force is low. Finally, even if all the above conditions are not met, the family may be poor if the working family members realize only a small proportion of their potential qualification in the jobs.

The level of poverty of a given family also depends on the degree of correlation of all these factors. A family with a high unemployment rate and high dependency ratio and whose members have low value for all the others parameters will certainly be poor, unless the amount of transfers it receives is high. On the other hand, if a high unemployment rate is accompanied by high average levels of the other parameters, the family may not be poor. Thus, poverty can be caused by any one and by a combination of the above variables.

The causation in the above equation may not be unidirectional, in the sense that the fact that a family is poor may result in low (or high) levels of the above variables. For example, the members of a poor family have, in general, less opportunity to improve their qualifications than those of a non-poor family. This lack of opportunity may create a vicious circle of poverty, in which poverty today may result in poverty tomorrow. The authors will have more to say about this below.

Active labour market policies can affect the unemployment rate, the bargaining power of workers, the qualification of the labour force and the extent to which this qualification is effectively realized in the job. Some policies affect one of the variables, while others affect more than one. Another important fact is that these variables are often correlated. For example, in developing countries, high quality workers tend to have a high bargaining power, and vice-versa. The following sections will be directed at analysing each of these policies.

At this point, a word about direct income transfers is important. Direct income transfers to poor families increase a family's per capita income and, as such, have a direct effect on poverty levels. Transfers can be a very important policy instrument to alleviate poverty in the short run and in emergency situations. However, although transfers are important in many cases, this paper will not consider them unless they affect one or many of the above variables which work together to determine the family's per capita income.

III. Policies directed at reducing unemployment

Policies which primarily influence aggregate demand for labour will not be considered in this chapter. These policies are, in general, classified as macro-economic, industrial or trade policies. Thus, only those policies which are strictly related to the labour markets and, among them, those directed at generating employment to the poor, will be considered.

This chapter first considers those policies designed to generate employment through Special Public Works Programmes which build public facilities using labour-intensive technology. As the product generated is in general non-tradable, the discount rate, the "price of time", is a very important decision variable which affects the choice of technology. If time is "expensive" so that the facilities must be built fast, the choice of technology tends to narrow down to capital-intensive technologies. On the other hand, if the discount rate is small, that is, time is less important, more labour-intensive technologies can be used. The problem here is the trade-off between construction time and employment generation.

A good example of how the discount rate can be an important variable in the choice of technology was the construction of a water canal in one of the poorest Brazilian states, Ceará, in 1993. This 118 kilometre long canal, built to bring water from Jaguaribe river to the capital city of Fortaleza, was constructed in 90 days. Since the local producers could not supply equipment and materials in the time required, the state imported them from other countries and from other states of Brazil. The construction project employed 5,000 workers. The total cost of the project — US$48 million — represented close to US$10,000 of investment per employment generated, or more than US$3,000 a month. As the canal had to be built in 90 days, capital-intensive technology had to be used, and the employment created was both minor and expensive. Further, as equipment and raw materials had to be imported from other regions, the indirect effect was also smaller than it could have been if locally-produced inputs had been used. From the point of view of generating employment for the poor and, thus, of poverty reduction in the short term, the choice of technology was a poor one, determined by the high price imputed to time.

Another relevant example is the construction of sewing systems in poor neighbourhoods. Such a project can be carried out using capital-intensive technology and little labour, or using less equipment and more labour. But the labour-intensive technology is certainly more time-intensive. Thus, if the sewing system has to be built in a short time — in other words, if the discount rate of time is high — capital-intensive technology will be chosen.

Thus, the main point is not to choose labour-intensive technology regardless of its cost effectiveness, but to use the discount rate as a policy variable to make the technological choice. The "price of time" is an imputed price and a policy decision variable in the case of public facilities construction, which is a non-tradable, non-competitive good. Thus, in these cases, the real choice is between employment generation and construction time.

The effect of these policies can be increased if they are planned and executed at the local level, as the water canal example above suggests. In general, centralized decision-making is, in general, more influenced by better organized and financially stronger interest groups than by small local enterprises, which tend to use a more labour- and time-intensive technology. Thus, decentralization of decision-making can be a useful instrument to increase labour absorption and reduce poverty through Special Public Works Programmes.

Many Latin American countries use Special Public Works Programmes to reduce the negative effects of structural adjustment programmes on the poor. Countries like Bolivia (*Fondo Social de Emergencia*), Mexico (PRONASOL), Honduras (*Fondo Hondureño de Inversión Social*), among others, introduced this kind of programme during the adjustment period to reduce the rate of unemployment and increase political support for the adjustment process. The budget of such programmes is centrally decided, but executed (i.e. regarding what to construct and how) at a very decentralized level [Martínez & Wurgaft, 1992].

Special Public Works Programmes can be a powerful instrument to reduce poverty generated by transitory unemployment. But, by themselves, they are not effective to reduce structural poverty. Rather they must be combined with other instruments designed to increase the permanent capacity of labour to generate income, that is, to increase the productivity of the jobs in the long run. This can be done through different mechanisms.

First, if productive infrastructure is built (e.g. local roads, sewing systems, water supply schemes, irrigation canals, electrical supply networks, etc.), marginal productivity of labour will also increase through an increase in the overall productivity of the system. Improved infrastructure creates a number of side effects, such as reduction in sickness, lower transport costs and thus a heightened information network, better quality of the land that is being used through irrigation, the use of more modern and efficient technology through the introduction of electricity, etc.

In the canal example given above, if the canal water is eventually available through irrigation canals to nearby farms so that the effect of future droughts is reduced and land productivity is increased, there will be a permanent reduction in poverty levels in the region.

As will be seen in the next section, Special Public Works Programmes can also be used to increase the quality of the labour force and thus to reduce structural poverty.

It is important that Special Public Works Programmes avoid employing mainly young school-age workers (10-to-17-year-old persons). In general, given the high poverty levels and the fact that many of these programmes pay less than the minimum wage and do not provide social benefits to workers, the increase in labour demand generates an increase in labour supply of the younger members of the family, reducing the dependency ratio. Although employment can reduce poverty in the short term, there is a risk of reducing labour qualifications and thus increasing poverty in the long run by taking children out of school. Thus, the programme should avoid the employment of very young people.

This is an example of an active labour market policy which could affect the dependency ratio, in this case, with negative long-term effects. If possible, these programmes should pay the minimum wage and social benefits as well so as to make them more attractive to older workers.

Thus, Special Public Works Programmes can reduce poverty not only through a short-term reduction in the rate of unemployment, but also through an increase in productivity and even an increase in the effort effectively supplied by labour if the product being built, like infrastructure and irrigation canals, increases the overall productivity of the system.

A second set of policies which could create jobs are those directed at improving the information flow between employers and workers. In general, labour markets have information and transaction costs. The problem is not only to find a worker or a job, but also to choose among different workers and different jobs. Thus, public employment services should be able to provide not only a list of vacancies and potential employable workers for these vacancies. They should also be able to provide information about the kind of jobs and the degree of qualification of the workers available.

This is particularly important for small and micro-enterprises, since many of these costs are fixed and thus tend to decline, per unit of employment generated, as the number of workers to be employed increases. In big firms, the selection process is part of the task of the Human Resources Departments, which uses newspaper advertisements, formal and informal contacts with training and educational institutions, and sophisticated and expensive selection instruments to select the workers. For small and micro-enterprises with limited financial resources and a small number of employees, it is too expensive to create this structure. Such companies tend to select their workers on the basis of informal contacts with other small and micro-enterprises and through a probation period. The result is a high rate of turnover, low productivity and low wages.

Public employment services should work in close collaboration with training institutions to provide information on the kind of occupations whose demand is increasing and declining. They should also develop a counselling service to the unemployed workers on the kind of retraining they should undertake to increase their employability. This is particularly important in structural adjustments periods when the structure of the demand for labour is changing and there is a high rate of obsolescence of human capital, mainly specific human capital, of the workers.

IV. Policies directed at improving the quality of jobs in the economy

In most countries, a large proportion of the working poor are employed in small and micro-enterprises or are self-employed; these are the main generators of employment for this group. Thus, policies which increase the quality of the jobs supplied by these enterprises are important tools to increase the income of the poor and thus to reduce poverty.

One policy that could be used to reach this objective is to facilitate access to credit for these firms. In general, for lack of collateral, they have little access to credit in the formal credit market. As a result they are exposed to very high interest rates in the informal credit markets, which reduces their rate of investment and thus the quality of the jobs they offer.

Thus, changes in commercial banking lending patterns (be they public or private banks) may be an important instrument to increase credit availability to small and micro-enterprises. One example of a change which could have substantial influence is lending on the basis of expected income generated by the project, not just on the basis of collateral. If the expected income of the project is high, credit should be provided.

This factor is compounded by the deficiencies in management in these enterprises. Thus, technical assistance programmes to allow them to use efficiently the credit supplied can be of great importance to reduce loan defaults and increase the survivor capacity of these firms. Key institutional programmes include services to small enterprises in the areas of administration, financing, accounting, marketing and quality control.

Three examples of programmes now in operation in Latin American countries are a global credit programme for small and micro-enterprises by the Central Bank of Costa Rica, including credit and technical assistance components at a total programme cost of US$12.5 million; the Mexican *Empresas Solidaridad*; and the FONDOMICRO in the Dominican Republic [ILO, 1992; PRONASOL, 1993]. The first two are government programmes, while the third is purely private.

In the first programme, "the objective is to facilitate the access of small and micro-enterprises to credit assistance facilities through viable institutions in accordance with market rules and mechanisms and to secure technology transfer to interested and efficient intermediary financial institutions" [ILO, 1992]. The second is a programme directed at financing viable and profitable productive projects that have no other sources of financing. The support includes credit and direct state participation in the project, as well as technical assistance. The objective is to increase the rate of creation of community-based enterprises, with direct government participation in the capital of the firms (up to 35 per cent of the total capital of the firm). The profits earned are divided between the entrepreneur and *Empresas Solidaridad* in proportion to the latter's participation in the capital of the project. Finally, the third programme is run by a private organization which provides credit directly to small and micro enterprises at market interest rate.

The importance of small and micro-enterprises is increasing due to the downgrading and out-sourcing practices of big firms which are part of the technological changes implemented by big industrial and service firms in developed as well as in developing countries. By this process, big firms buy from outside suppliers many services and products which were previously produced internally. The result can be a reduction in working standards, since big firms tend to have better working relations than small firms. It can also increase informality in the labour market, reduce quality of employment generated and thus increase poverty levels.

To avoid these undesired effects, and to guarantee that the process effectively increases productivity and competitiveness, it is very important that the subcontracted firms can provide products with high quality and that working conditions do not deteriorate during the process. This will mean an upgrading of small firms' technology and labour practices. Programmes which provide financing for this upgrading, which includes the training of small firm employees and owners to improve the quality of the services and products supplied, information on technological choices, and on labour standards, are of key importance.

Due to fixed costs and externalities, this objective can be reached more easily by encouraging the creation of small and micro-enterprise networks. These networks could be organized on the basis of a common buyer of the products generated by the small firms when they are suppliers of components or inputs for big firms, or on a sectoral basis, putting together small firms producing similar products. Cooperative arrangements among small firms, to increase the degree of specialization, to divide training and selection costs of workers and owners, and to reduce the unit costs of technological development, are greatly facilitated by these networks.

It is very important, to avoid the inadvertent increase of informalization and poverty, that some kind of "labour standard conditionality" is implemented by the programme for those firms that have access to the credit. Formalization of the workers and good working conditions in the firms are two examples of the kind of conditionality suggested here. Labour standard conditionality can also be important in creating labour relations conducive to faster productivity growth.

One example of such a programme is being implemented in Brazil by SEBRAE, an employer organization, which provides financial support to firms that are undergoing a process of downgrading of activities. The programme is designed by the firms with training institutions, and financed by SEBRAE. It also provides direct financing to small and micro-enterprises to improve management practices and product quality.

V. Policies directed at improving the quality of the labour force

A low-quality labour force is one of the main generators of poverty. As the marginal productivity of labour is small not only are wages low, but workers also have low bargaining power. Policies to increase the quality of the labour force supplied by the poor are related to education and training. Some of them are linked to small and micro-enterprises. Others are related to the low qualification level of the poor.

Special Public Works Programmes can be an important catalyst for increasing the quality of the labour force through on-the-job training. It is common in many countries to have national training institutions (like SENAI and SENAC in Brazil, INFOTEP in the Dominican Republic and INA in Costa Rica), many of them financed through a payroll tax. These institutions could be mobilized to provide the courses and all firms participating in the programme should be encouraged to provide on-the-job training to the employed labour force during the duration of the programme. If this is done, besides generating employment in the short term, the programme will result in an increase in the quality of the labour force in the long term.

Also, as unemployment has as one of its consequences the rapid obsolescence of the human capital of the workers, mainly of specific human capital, it is of key importance that vocational training be extended to the unemployed and underemployed. Here, the experience of many countries has shown that the focus of the programmes should be on the development of basic cognitive skills of the unemployed workers and not on specific training only. Basic cognitive skills are important to increase the overall qualification of workers, mainly of the poor, who often have a low educational level. Again, during structural adjustment periods, when there is a high level of uncertainty about the future structure of labour demand, basic cognitive skills are more important than specific skills to increase the employability of the workers.

Another set of policies that should be considered are those related to small and micro-enterprises. Besides having a low rate of investment, as seen in the previous section, small and micro-enterprises are also characterized by low investment in their labour force. Training programmes are expensive and the private rate of return to the firm tends to be smaller than the social rate of return due to problems of property rights. Training becomes embodied in the worker and, unless it is very specific training, the firm will lose its investment if the worker leaves the firm. As financial capital is in short supply for these firms, they under-invest in their labour force.

If the problem of property rights in training is important, the natural way to overcome this problem is to provide these services on a social basis. Special programmes to provide on-the-job training to workers in small and micro-enterprises through national training institutions can play an important role in this process. Further, if public employment services could work in close contact with training institutions, as suggested above, the costs of employment generation would be greatly reduced and the productivity of labour increased. Both effects would work in the direction of increasing wages and reducing poverty levels.

The low level of general education is also an important determinant of poverty. This deficiency can be caused by poverty itself as well as by the low quality of the public basic education system in many developing countries. Poverty itself affects the general level of qualification of the poor for the simple reason that, although basic public education is free, the cost to poor people to remain in school is very high. This cost is divided into monetary costs, such as transport, school materials, clothes, etc., and the "opportunity cost" of being in school as opposed to earning income in the labour market.

The problem is that the opportunity cost of staying in school tends to be very high and increases with age. In many countries, the children of poor families enter the labour market very early since their income is of key importance to the family's living standard in the present. As the level of per capita income of the family is too low, the contribution that the children can make to total family income is relatively high, although their income levels are low. In Brazil, for example, close to 20 per cent of children 10 to 14 years of age of poor families (families with per-capita monthly income of US$80 or less) work. Even more important, of those children in the above age class that do work, close to 50 per cent work 40 hours or more per week. Thus, school is certainly a second or third priority for these children.

The result is very high repeat rates and absenteeism rates from the school system. Thus, not only do the children of poor families enter the labour market very early, with few qualifications, but they also have little chance to improve their qualification levels. As they will be the non-qualified labour force of the future, their wages will be low. So, poverty today generates poverty tomorrow and this vicious circle is certainly a very important generator of poverty in many countries. Thus, reducing the opportunity cost of staying in school is an important way to reduce future poverty.

One policy which could have this effect is to pay a fixed amount per family (or per mother) to keep all their young members in a public school up to a certain age. This policy will reduce the opportunity cost of being in school and increase school attendance and, as a result, the level of general qualification of the children of poor families. A kind of income transfer, this policy can reduce poverty in the present and, at the same time, increase the productivity of the poor and thereby reduce poverty in the future.

The above argument is directly related to the non-existence of a credit market for education. If the rate of return of education is greater than the rate of interest, the provision of educational credit will increase the demand for education by the poor, since the gains in future income will be higher than the cost of the credit. Thus, educational credit can be a powerful instrument to increase qualification among the poor.

Also, many of the policies to increase the quality of the educational system can have as a by-product an increase in the opportunity cost for the families of keeping their children in schools. Examples are the introduction of full-time school for the poor, or those increases in quality which are intensive in terms of the time of the children (and of the family) outside the schools. These policies, as they increase the time children must dedicate to their qualification, can have as a negative effect the reduction of the time the children of poor families stay in the school system. This is because the opportunity cost, for these children, of being in school is very high. Thus, it is important that the policies directed at increasing the quality of the educational system also reduce the opportunity cost of being in school. Examples are those policies which induce the teachers to help the students to learn in class and rely minimally on homework, or those policies which makes it easier for the children to learn through special pedagogical methods or the provision of good school materials, etc.

VI. Bargaining power, work effort and institutional framework

This area is possibly the one where there is the least consensus on which policies are effective in reducing poverty. There are two main problems in this context. First, the poor, in general, are "outsiders" as regards union structure and, for this reason, have little bargaining power. Second, many analysts suggest that every programme designed to protect workers from labour market outcomes (be they unemployment or low wages) will have as by-products a reduction in work incentives and/or some kind of misallocation of resources, thus reducing productivity and growth and increasing unemployment. The evidence on these two points is not at all conclusive and the dispute is still to be solved [Blank & Freeman, 1993].

The first problem is related to the question of how to reduce the variance of bargaining power in society. If some groups have high bargaining power while others are weak, there can be an incentive to rent-seeking behaviour on the part of the stronger groups, reducing the income of the weaker and, if this last group is poor, thus increasing poverty.

Bargaining power is intimately related to the structure of capital/labour relations and thus to the institutional and legislative framework which organizes collective and individual bargaining between employers and workers, workers' protection against possible unfair employers' practices, the mechanisms to resolve collective and individual conflicts, etc.

One particularly important aspect is the degree of centralization or decentralization of collective bargaining. The evidence from developed countries has shown that centralized collective bargaining tends to generate a more egalitarian wage structure and less poverty, as compared to decentralized collective bargaining.[3] If collective bargaining is centralized, workers' bargaining power increases for all workers, the unions' constituency is more encompassing, including those groups of workers which would have little bargaining power if they had to negotiate alone. Thus, the probability of rent-seeking behaviour is reduced.

But many analysts point out that, as centralized collective bargaining strengthens the workers' position, it can limit the employers' ability to adjust to the changing economic environment by creating rigidities in wages, by reducing employers' ability to cut employment in the face of short-term shocks and by slowing labour reallocation. As a result, fewer jobs will be created, increasing the rate of unemployment and having a negative effect on poverty levels (see, among others, Lindbeck & Snower [1990]).

But arguments in favour of social protection are also present in the literature. One line of argument stresses the role of these programmes in enhancing human capital and productivity in the labour market. "From a human capital perspective, social protection programmes could create long-

---

[3] For evidence see Blank & Freeman [1993] and *Quarterly Journal of Economics*, Vol. 17, No. 1, Feb. 1992.

term incentives for employers and workers to invest in training. For instance, laws that limit dismissal might induce employers to invest more in worker training, since they create the long-term attachment that makes investment in specific skills profitable" [Blank & Freeman, 1993, p. 17].

Although it is not possible with the available evidence to decide which of the above lines of arguments is the more important, the evidence tends to show that countries with very centralized collective bargaining and with economy-wide coordination mechanisms to determine wages are more egalitarian and have less poverty than countries with decentralized collective bargaining. Also, countries with a more comprehensive system of worker protection tend to have higher unemployment rates but higher rates of growth in labour productivity than countries with more market-oriented institutional structures, unless the worker protection institutions are accompanied by other forms of flexibility in the labour markets.[4]

Thus, it can be stated at this point that an increase in the bargaining power of workers, if it implies more protection, should be accompanied by changes in market institutions which allow for more flexibility in other dimensions of the labour markets to avoid an increase in unemployment.

Here, the question of the institutional framework and work effort is of key importance. Given the special characteristics of the labour market, where moral hazard and "prisoners' dilemmas" are very common, the amount of effort the worker gives on the job will depend on the structure of the capital-labour relations and the institutional framework. Some examples of this relation will be useful to clarify this point.

One example is the "prisoners' dilemma" generated by authoritarian employer-worker relations.[5]

Suppose the worker produces y units of a good per unit of time, if he works and has disutility $d < w$. If he does not work, he produces nothing, with no subjective cost. The employer pays wages $w < y$. Assume the power balance and institutions are such that, if the employer accuses the worker of shirking, he can decide unilaterally to pay or not to pay the wage. There is no possibility of checking whether such an accusation is right or wrong. The matrix below shows the payoffs of the worker and the employer:

---

[4] A good discussion on the evidence is summarized in Blank & Freeman [1993]. See also Soskice [1990].

[5] This example is taken from Azam [1989], although in this paper the example is used to make a different point.

Worker

		work	*not work*
pay		y−w; w−d	−w ; w
Employer			
accuse		y; −d	0;0

From the above matrix, under this "dilemma", the most likely strategy for the worker and for the employer is not to work and not to pay, respectively. To see this, suppose the worker believes the employer will pay. If that is so, if he works, he will get w−d and if he does not work he will get w. Thus, the best for him is not to work. Suppose, instead, the worker believes the employer is not going to pay. If he works, his pay-off will be −d and if he does not work it will be 0. So the best option for him is not to work, regardless of what he expects the employer will do.

Now take the employer. Suppose he believes the worker is really working. If he pays, his pay-off will be y−w, and if he does not pay it will be y. So, the best strategy for him is not to pay in this case. Now suppose he believes the worker did not work. If he pays he will gain −w, and if he does not pay he will gain 0. So the best strategy for him is not to pay, regardless what he believes the worker has done. So not to work and not to pay is the most likely strategy for both agents.

But if the worker knew in advance that the employer would pay, and the employer knew that the worker would work, the final result would be better for both agents. What this simple example shows is that the threat of non-payment of due wages is not an effective instrument to increase work effort. To render this example more practical, such a threat could be extended, along a continuum of disciplinary procedures, to the threat of dismissal (or lock-out in case of collective effort being withheld).

Note that if the game is repeated many times, cooperation would result in the efficient outcome. Thus, institutions which increase the length of the work contract and thus increase the flow of information and cooperation between the agents can be powerful instruments to increase labour effort and thus productivity.

Another interesting example is related to unemployment insurance and the incentive to employment. Unemployment insurance has been blamed by many analysts as an institution which reduces the incentives the workers have to search and accept employment, thus reducing the supply of labour. The importance of this argument for developing countries is difficult to assess, since most of them do not have unemployment insurance and there are very few studies of the effects of this mechanism in those countries that do have it.

In one case, Brazil, the effect does not seem to go in a different direction. Brazil went through two important recessions, in 1981-1984 and 1990-1992. In the first period, the country had no unemployment insurance. However, this was introduced in 1986 and so was present in the second recession. Thus, theoretically, unemployment would be expected to be a more important adjustment variable in the second episode than in the first. Primary data suggest that the opposite was the case. In the first recession, unemployment increased much more than in the second, while underemployment increased much more in the 1990s recession than in the 1980s recession. Thus, at least in this case, unemployment insurance did not seem to have induced workers to stay unemployed longer.

There are many explanations for the above observed behaviour, but one is especially interesting in the context of this work. In the Brazilian unemployment insurance programme the eligible worker receives a fixed benefit for four months. The government makes very little effort to check whether the worker is effectively looking for a new job or if he has found a job during this period. If he finds a formal job, it is possible, but with low probability, that he will lose the benefit. For the worker, this means that if he finds a job during this period, he will continue to receive the unemployment insurance, plus the wage of the new job. If the new job is in the informal sector, the government has no way to check and thus he is likely to receive both the unemployment insurance and the wage in the informal work. Thus, the benefit is similar to a money transfer for four months to the person made unemployed in a given month. It is not surprising that unemployed workers did not reduce their labour supply while unemployed.

But it is important to note that, in this case, workers have an incentive to take short-term work contracts (although there are restrictions on the number of times a given worker can be eligible for unemployment insurance during a period of two years), provided they are able to get a new job easily when fired. By the same token, the firms have an incentive to informalize their labour force, since informalization implies fewer social taxes, and the workers have an incentive to accept this informalization, since they can increase their income. Thus, the possible behaviour of workers who are in the time limit to become eligible for the unemployment insurance programme, will be to look for a new job while still employed, increasing the turnover rate in the economy, reducing work effort on the job and reducing training and human capital investment. Also, there is an additional incentive to increase the informalization of the labour market, and not to increase unemployment.

This example points to the importance of the institutional design to generate the desired incentives. If workers stop receiving the unemployment insurance benefit when they find a new job, there will be less incentive to look for another job while the benefit is being paid. To attract these workers, employers will have to offer higher real wages and better working conditions than if there was no unemployment insurance. In other words, the bargaining power of the workers increases with such an unemployment insurance mechanism. Note that all workers, including those employed, will have increased bargaining power, since there is a reduction of labour supply. Provided the employed workers and the employers agree to pay the costs of the unemployment insurance programme, this will certainly result in reduction in poverty levels.

On the other hand, if the unemployment insurance mechanism is such that the worker can find another job *and* maintain the unemployment benefit if the new job is in the informal labour market, there will be an incentive to increase the degree of informalization and a reduction in the length of the labour contract. The result will be less human capital investment and training.

A third example is related to lay-off compensation. Many countries have legislation which provides monetary compensation for the worker when he is laid off. Often, this compensation is directly proportional to the time the worker was employed in the firm. This kind of institution may provide incentives for the workers in jobs without clear promotion opportunities, for instance, to seek dismissal which is contrary to the spirit of the regulation. For these workers, being laid off means an immediate, and even substantial, income flow, depending on how long they have held their jobs.

In periods of recession, the probability of getting another job is smaller and consequently the worker has less incentive to seek to be laid off. However, as the economy grows and the probability of getting another job quickly increases, the optimum strategy is to seek to be laid off, reducing the amount of effort dedicated to the current job and consequently reducing productivity. The optimum strategy is to search whilst in a job, so that the chances of getting another job quickly are maximized. The final result will certainly be a considerable decrease in productivity in the current job.

If workers have an incentive to seek dismissal as soon as possible, the firm, on the other hand, has every incentive to exploit the workers as much as possible since no long-term relationship is being sought. In particular, neither firms nor workers have any incentive in firm-specific human capital, since the imminent rupture of the relationship does not make this investment profitable. By the same token, firms have no incentive to provide on-the-job training for their workers.

The final result of such a process is low-quality jobs, under-utilized workers and a low-productivity labour force, with substantial effects on poverty.

It is important to note that as there are social costs associated with laying off workers. Firms that ignore these costs and lay off workers too often should be penalized. But, if the above incentive is to be avoided, this penalization should not be appropriated by the dismissed worker. It would be better if it is used to finance an unemployment insurance programme, or a pension fund for the workers, for example.

The purpose of the above examples is to point out the importance of institutions in determining the incentive structure and, thus, the work effort. As productivity depends on these variables, the effect on poverty levels can be very important. Given the above considerations, it is clear that institutions are non-market mechanisms which are used by societies to influence the behaviour of agents and other institutions. If that is so, we should first ask what behaviour we want our labour market institutions to induce. Although this question could be answered in different ways, we would like to suggest that labour market institutions should induce behaviour which would:

— increase labour productivity;
— increase labour income;
— reduce the degree of inequality in society;
— avoid unemployment.

The second question is: Do labour market institutions which are directed at "protecting" workers induce behaviour which will generate these four outcomes? The answer to this question is, not necessarily. But then, why do we want to "protect" workers? In general, we want to protect workers because we think they are weaker in the capital-labour relation. In other words, there is a power asymmetry between employers and workers and so, to avoid unfair labour practices, the workers should be protected.

But, if that is the case, we should try to develop labour market institutions which increase the power of labour, as compared with that of employers and, at the same time, induce the behaviour that we are looking for. Only if labour is stronger and thus less uncertain about the future, can we expect it to be more flexible and expect flexibility not to degenerate into more precarious labour relations. If that is possible, and we are not convinced that this is the case, this is certainly a more effective way to design labour market institutions. This approach to labour market institutions would be a powerful complement to the usual approach of mere "protection" of workers against situations of adverse market and working conditions.

Finally, it is important to consider that, for very poor workers, the incentive to work is directly related to nutrition and health considerations. Programmes which provide food and health care directly to poor workers can have important effects on the amount of effort they can provide on the job.

VII. Conclusions

This chapter analyses how different labour market policies can be used to reduce poverty. Four set of policies were analysed. First, policies to increase the rate of employment generation; second, policies which could result in an increase in the quality of the employment; third, policies to improve the quality of the labour force supplied by the poor; and, finally, policies which would increase the amount of effort effectively put in by workers in the job. All these policies can be of great importance in reducing poverty.

Among the first group, the key policy instrument to help increase employment generation is the "price of time" through Special Public Works Programmes. It is argued that, if time is very expensive, the discount rate is high and capital-intensive technologies will be chosen, thereby reducing the generation of employment. On the other hand, if time is less expensive, labour-intensive technologies could be used.

It is also suggested that these programmes should concentrate on the construction of productive infrastructures, irrigation canals, electricity distribution networks, etc., which could have as a result an increase in the productivity of the economic system and long-term effects on poverty levels.

Another policy instrument which can increase the rate of employment generation is the reduction of transaction and information costs through public employment systems. This is particularly important to small and micro-enterprises, since the fixed costs to develop information system tend to be high for these firms.

The second set of policies, designed to improve the quality of the employment generated, include the development of networks of small and micro-enterprises with the objective of improving their capacity to invest in their labour force, and increase credit availability to these enterprises.

Third, there are those policies to improve the quality of the labour force, which includes incentives for on-the-job training, retraining of unemployed workers (mainly basic cognitive skills) and general education, mainly for the young. Here a policy to provide education credits, or a subsidy for poor families to keep their children in school longer, can be powerful instruments to improve the educational level of the poor.

Finally, the chapter analyses the effect of institutional arrangements on the bargaining power of workers, on workers' effort on the job and on productivity. Real wage growth depends on productivity and on bargaining power. Bargaining power will depend on the degree of unions organization and on the structure of collective bargaining, which is a result of the institutional framework. On the other hand, productivity growth will depend on the qualification of the labour force, improvement in the quality of jobs and incentives for workers to provide effort. Thus, institutions which create incentives for on-the-job training are very important. Institutions which induce long-term labour relations might cause employers to invest more in worker training, since they create the long-term attachment that makes investment in specific skills profitable, increases labour productivity and real wages and reduces poverty.

Given all this, the importance of the institutional framework cannot be overrated. So the design of institutions should be taken very seriously. It is thus suggested that institutions should be designed to induce labour market behaviour which would increase labour productivity, real wages, reduce inequality and avoid unemployment, instead of "protecting" workers. It is suggested that a possible alternative to labour protection is to design institutions which would result in an increase in labour's power in society so that protection is not necessary and, at the same time, induce the desired behaviour. Although it is not clear that it is possible (although some countries have been able to do so), it can be a better approach to reforming labour market institutions.

Bibliographical references

Azam, J.-P. 1989. "Recent developments in the DC literature on labour markets and the macroeconomy and their implications for LDCs", mimeo. CERDI, Université de Clermont-Ferrand.

Barros, R.; Camargo, J. M. 1993. "Poverty in Brazil: A challenge for the future", in Maria D'Alva G. Kinzo (ed.): *Brazil: The challenges of the 1990s*. London, Institute of Latin American Studies and British Academic Press.

—. 1993. "The determinants of the level of social welfare in Latin America", Interamerican Development Bank.

Blank, R. M.; Freeman, R. 1993. "Evaluating the connection between social protection and economic flexibility", NBER Working Paper No. 4338, Cambridge, USA.

International Labour Organization. 1992. "Stabilization, structural adjustment and social policies in Costa Rica: The role of compensatory programmes", Occasional Paper No. 1, Geneva.

Lindbech, A.; Snower, D. 1990. "Demand and supply-side policies and unemployment: policy implications of the insider-outsider approach", in Holmlund, B.; Loftgren, K.G. (eds.): *Unemployment and wage determination in Europe*. Oxford, Blackwell Ltd.

Martínez, D.; Wurgaft, J. 1992. "Fondos de inversión social: situación y perspectivas", mimeo. Santiago, PREALC/ILO.

Soskice, D. 1990. "Wage determination: The changing role of institutions in advanced industrialized countries", in *Oxford Review of Economic Policy* (Oxford, Oxford University Press), Vol. 6, No. 4, winter.

PRONASOL. 1993. "Notas sobre la experiencia de empresas de solidaridad", mimeo.

Quarterly Journal of Economics (Cambridge). 1992, Vol. 17, No. 1, February.

3 Labour market policies, vulnerable groups and poverty

Selected Countries
I32
J68

Richard Anker[1]

I. Introduction

Labour market policies and poverty are both a central focus of ILO policy and these are closely linked to policies for vulnerable groups. Indeed, a 1992 paper prepared for the Committee on Employment of the Governing Body of the ILO defines active labour market policies as policies "to provide work to, or increase the employability of, people with certain disadvantages in the labour market" [ILO, 1992a]. While a subsequent 1993 Employment Committee report for the ILO Governing Body [ILO, 1993] rightly broadens the scope and purpose of active labour market policies to encompass all workers, and not mainly disadvantaged workers, there can be little disagreement that disadvantaged groups are an important focus of labour market policies. This emphasis takes on added relevance for poverty issues, since the main productive asset available to the poor is their own under-compensated labour power.

The situation faced by vulnerable groups varies greatly around the world due, for example, to differing macro-economic and labour market conditions and policies; labour market institutions; availability of social safety nets; family structure and strength of the extended family; levels of education and human capital; degree of formalization of the labour market and size of the so-called informal sector; size of the government and its ability to fund labour market programmes and enforce labour laws and regulations.

A typical categorization of labour markets is to divide the world into three groups. Industrialized or OECD countries have large formal labour markets; major problems with open unemployment; significant government budgets and commitments to labour market programmes, laws and

---

[1] International Labour Office, Geneva.

regulations. Transition economies have many of the same characteristics as OECD countries (e.g. high degree of formalization of labour markets; relatively high labour force participation rates for women and relatively low participation rates for children and older persons; and significant government intervention in the labour market), but are in the process of developing their labour market institutions and laws and are now experiencing a rapid transformation towards a market economy with large increases in open unemployment together with reductions in government budgets and social expenditures. Developing countries are generally depicted as having relatively high poverty rates; extended families which often — but not always — help to spread the pains of poverty by taking care of family members; and labour markets which are largely informal in nature and not very amenable to labour market policies; and governments which generally do not have the financial or administrative means to implement labour market programmes or enforce labour market laws and regulations.

These broad sketches of OECD, transition economies and developing countries are, like most generalizations, oversimplifications. It is especially important to recognize that there is an increasing convergence in labour market conditions throughout the world as a result of the trend towards globalization of the economy. OECD countries are experiencing a rapid growth in service sector jobs and a decrease in manufacturing sector jobs; an increase in casual work contracts and part-time employment (in the European Union, for example, 30 per cent of all women workers are in part-time employment [CCE, 1992]; an increase in the wage gap between skilled and unskilled workers; and an increase in so-called labour market flexibility. In contrast, a number of developing countries (the newly industrializing countries (NICs) in East Asia and Latin America) now have sizeable formal sectors, and open unemployment is a major problem associated with poverty [Rodgers, 1989]. Unfortunately, another set of developing countries, most obviously in Africa, are not developing, as they have been left outside of the increasingly interlinked global economy.

With this broad sketch of country types as a background, the remainder of this chapter deals with labour market-related poverty issues for vulnerable groups. First, there is a discussion of the concept and measurement of poverty — and its implications for labour market policies; in particular, how to reconcile what is essentially a household-level approach to poverty with what is essentially an individual- or group-level approach to labour market policies. Secondly, there is a discussion of the terms "*vulnerable groups*" and "*disadvantaged groups*" and why persons in these groups need labour market policies in the context of poverty alleviation. Thirdly, we discuss the objectives and boundaries of labour market policies for different types of economies and societies and what this implies for vulnerable groups. This includes a brief discussion of the extent to which poverty groups are similar in the world (determined mainly by physical and demographic characteristics, such as age, sex, race, disability, and ethnicity) and/or the extent to which they are created by labour market functioning and economic conditions. This also includes discussions of the need for poverty-oriented policies to go beyond traditional interpretations of labour market policies to include economic, social and family policies; to take into consideration long-run and short-run aspects of vulnerability; to consider trade-offs and complementarities between the equity, efficiency and growth objectives of active labour market policies; and the importance for vulnerable groups of a social justice objective. Finally, there are discussions of poverty-oriented labour market policies in the context of three important "traditional" vulnerable groups — children, women and the disabled.

II. What is poverty? Implications for poverty-oriented labour market policies

Poverty is generally conceptualized and measured at the household level. Typically, poverty lines are established on the basis of income required for a typical size household to purchase a basic food basket with minimum levels of proteins and calories.[2,3] There is much to recommend in this approach. It is "relatively" easy to measure and track household income or consumption; it has an appealing quantitative assuredness; and it captures the basic concept of survival at a minimum level. It also allows for the fact that households engage in complex survival strategies, both in terms of their allocation of labour between market and non-market activities as well as in terms of their sharing of income or consumption.

---

[2] Composition of the basic food basket is usually adapted to the local situation and dietary habits of the poor. Thus, in some Latin American and African countries, the basic staple food might be maize, while in certain Asian countries the basic staple food might be pulses or rice.

[3] Once the cost of the basic food basket is established, the poverty line (or minimum income line) is estimated by multiplying this cost by a prescribed factor. It is interesting to note that this multiplier varies greatly around the world from 1.20 in India (cited in Streeten [1994]), to 1.75-2.00 and 2.00-2.50 in Latin America (cited in Sainz [1994] for ECLA and in Fields [1994] for IDB), to 3.00 for the USA.

For labour market policies, however, a household-based income or consumption concept of poverty leaves much to be desired and can even lead to confusion. First, labour market policies are typically oriented toward types or groups of individuals with particular characteristics (e.g. women, children, elderly, unemployed, etc. — see Section IV below for a fuller discussion on this) and not towards particular types of households (although female-headed households are often an exception). Secondly, household income (below or near the poverty line) tells only part of the story about vulnerability; since income varies over the year and across the years the availability of savings or assets which can be drawn upon in times of need, is important. Thirdly, the extent to which households have multiple income sources or are dependent on only one, perhaps risky, source of income is ignored. Fourthly, access to public goods (e.g. crèches, safe water, sewage treatment) and non-economic outcome measures (e.g. life expectancy, literacy) are also ignored in a purely income-based measure of poverty,[4] even though they are essential aspects of well-being and can be important for disadvantaged groups in helping them to cope with difficult labour market conditions.[5] Fifthly, no consideration is paid to the intra-household allocation of assets or consumption. Yet, households are often quite inequitable in how they allocate resources to family members, with women often suffering [Khan, Anker et al, 1992; Haddad & Kanbar, 1990]. Sixthly, it is implicitly (and wrongly) assumed that the extended family is not only an efficient and equitable allocator, but also that household structures are immutable. Nevertheless, with urbanization and development, the extended family becomes weaker; this has major implications for the poverty of various vulnerable groups such as older persons, disabled and separated women, especially during the period when the extended family has significantly

---

[4] There are alternative measures of poverty which take into consideration the extent to which basic needs are being met, such as access to clean water, health care, sewage treatment and disposal, safe environment, adequate housing, and schools [Boltvinik, 1994]. Also outcome variables are sometimes used, such as life expectancy, literacy and infant mortality [United Nations: *Human Development Reports*]. A major difficulty with these approaches is that they are arbitrary regarding different dimensions of poverty and how these are aggregated into one poverty measure [van der Hoeven & Anker, 1994].

[5] These factors often seriously constrain poor persons from earning an adequate income and becoming fully integrated into the labour market. Inadequate health services, poor housing conditions, unsafe water and lack of sewage treatment, for example, negatively affect health and this in turn affects labour productivity and absences from work. These factors also fall particularly hard on women who are usually responsible for household work (including sometimes having to spend long hours getting water, fuel, etc.) and caring for other household members (infants, children, elderly and sick).

weakened and the government does not yet have adequate safety nets or effective labour market policies to assist vulnerable groups. Finally, female-headed households are quite common at all levels of development and this has major implications for the poverty of women and children (in Chile, for example, 60 per cent of female-headed households are poor).

The above discussion implies that rather than concentrating exclusively on measuring poverty, using aggregate and household-level measures of income and consumption as at present, more use (particularly in organizations such as the ILO) should be made of labour market-related measures of poverty. This could include indicators of overall labour market conditions in terms of: employment (such as unemployment rates and extent of part-time and precarious jobs in industrialized and transition countries; and relative size of the informal sector and proportion of marginal self-employment in developing countries); wage rates for the poor, such as statutory minimum wage and market wage rates for typical unskilled workers (perhaps for unskilled service jobs in industrialized and transition countries and for unskilled construction and agricultural jobs in developing countries); the number of workers holding multiple jobs and/or having self-employed income-earning activities, to proxy for the extent to which complex survival strategies are required; the cost of basic food product(s) in relation to unskilled wage rates to help measure the real value of a poor person's wage within a poverty concept; and the number of workers with casual/temporary contracts to measure labour market vulnerability. There is considerable developmental work required in this area of poverty-related labour market indicators, especially for developing countries.

There is also a need to improve labour market information and evaluation in order to enhance our understanding of the effectiveness of labour market policies and programmes and thus increase our ability to identify and target individuals in poverty and in need of assistance — including use of rapid assessment methodologies [Bilsborrow et al., 1993]. Some recent efforts have been made on indicators by the ILO World Labour Report in its data annex; in PREALC's data bank; in EMPLOI's data centre and, of course, in ILO's ongoing statistical reporting, such as in the *Yearbook of Labour Statistics*. But clearly, much more needs to be done.

Where does the above discussion leave us in devising poverty-oriented labour market policies? Can the basically household-level concept for poverty be reconciled with the basically individual — or group — level concept for labour markets? Specifically, should poverty-oriented labour market policies take into consideration the income/poverty status of an individual's household in setting priorities, by using a household income conditionality criteria? This last question could be further elaborated at the group level. Should groups which come predominantly from non-poor, well-to-do households be excluded from a poverty-oriented labour market policies approach? Considering typical target groups for labour market policies, for example, this would imply that unemployed educated youth in developing countries should be excluded from a poverty-oriented labour market policy as most of them come from relatively well-off households. The author is inclined towards this view.[6] What about other typical target groups (such as women, the elderly, migrants) which have sizeable numbers residing in both non-poor and poor households; should household income status be taken into consideration in designing policy and targeting assistance? The author would not favour a strict use of such an approach. Not only would this not be feasible in most countries (due to lack of data), but also inappropriate. The definition and structure of households are malleable [Oppong & Abu, 1987]. In addition, too close a linkage would undoubtedly rebound against groups which might be viewed as secondary earners (e.g. women and the disabled in many countries). A more appropriate and straightforward approach would be to use appropriate labour market information to concentrate policy and programmes on those segments of vulnerable groups that are located in what have been identified as low-wage/low-income segments of the labour market, especially those also having insecure work "contracts" and unsafe working conditions.

III. What are disadvantaged and vulnerable groups?

The designations vulnerable group, disadvantaged group and target group are terms frequently used to identify people in need of assistance. Are there any differences in the meaning of these terms?[7] What do they imply for labour market policies; and how do they translate into poverty-oriented labour market policies and strategies? Indeed, why are certain

---

[6] This view does not detract from the fact that labour market policies for unemployed educated youth in developing countries are important for improving labour market functioning, promoting economic growth and reducing political tension.

[7] The terms *vulnerable* and *poverty* are also sometimes (incorrectly) used as if they are synonymous with *poverty*. "Vulnerable groups (are often said to) stand for the poor." Robert Chambers [1989], however, correctly distinguishes between them. "Poverty can be reduced by borrowing and investing but such debt makes households more vulnerable. There are trade-offs between poverty and vulnerability or between security and income." [Streeten, 1994a].

groups believed to be in need of assistance in the labour market and how does this need relate to poverty or household income status?

Webster's Dictionary [1987] defines *vulnerable* as "open to attack, hurt or injury" and *disadvantaged* as "economically deprived or handicapped people or groups of people". For our purposes, both definitions imply a disadvantage in the labour market in terms of, for example, gaining access to the labour market and so getting work; and once in the labour market, finding well-paying, non-exploitative work with decent working conditions or employment security. The perspective taken in the ILO framework paper to this Symposium [ILO, 1993] is that disadvantage or vulnerability relates to inefficiency and inequity in the labour market, particularly in segmented labour markets. The terms of vulnerability and disadvantage then fit together nicely for a poverty-oriented labour market approach. The focus would be on groups which are in a disadvantaged position in the labour market and which at the same time are vulnerable to exploitation, either because they are poor or are vulnerable to becoming poor.

In devising policies for groups usually designated as vulnerable (e.g. women, children, disabled, the elderly, migrants, racial/ethnic groups, etc.), it is very important to take into consideration that they are very heterogeneous in terms of poverty status. While virtually all members in these groups face various forms of inequality and discrimination in the labour market, not all members are poor; and not even all child workers are poor. Some earn high incomes; others reside in high-income households. This again re-emphasizes the need to target particularly vulnerable subgroups within broadly-defined disadvantaged groups. For this kind of targeting, relevant and accurate labour market information is required. Very often such target subgroups will be at the intersection of different disadvantaged groups — for example, migrant women who are forced into prostitution, disabled elderly women who are without family support, and bonded child labourers who are living and working away from home.

In deciding on appropriate poverty-oriented labour market policies for disadvantaged groups, it is useful to know why people are disadvantaged or vulnerable in the labour market. Are they in this situation because of:

1. Characteristics which they bring to the labour market (e.g. less education; less skill or experience; ill health or physical handicaps; constraining household responsibility; culturally determined constraints).

2. How the labour market functions and has been functioning for some time (e.g. discrimination and/or occupational segregation of women,

the elderly and disabled; lack of access to credit, assets or technology; acceptance by society of child labour).

3. Macro-economic and labour trends (such as structural adjustment programmes; defence conversion; transition to market economy; recession; globalization of production) which exacerbates the situation faced by traditional disadvantaged groups and/or creates significant new disadvantaged groups such as long-term unemployed, persons in depressed localities, refugees and international migrants.

"Traditional" vulnerable or disadvantaged groups are generally distinguished by observable physical characteristics, such as race, ethnicity, disability, age and gender. Thus, typical disadvantaged groups for labour market policies are child labourers, youth, women, disabled and racial/ethnic/indigenous groups. Most of these groups are disadvantaged in the labour market in most countries, independent of political system, labour market institutions or development level. There are clearly universal aspects of human society and labour markets which are at least partly responsible for this disadvantaged position, implying that a package of social, political and labour market policies is required to address their disadvantaged position in the labour market. An interesting and relevant issue is how recent macro-economic changes are impacting on these traditional disadvantaged groups, and what should be done to ameliorate possible negative effects. In the so-called transition economies, for example, there is convincing evidence that disadvantaged groups have suffered most [Standing et al., 1992; Paukert, 1993]. For what one might call the new, "non-traditional" disadvantaged group, such as the long-term unemployed, different sets of policy packages are generally required, ones which are more time — and location — specific and which perhaps place less emphasis on social policy, as these new groups are created mainly by economic circumstances.

IV. Labour market policies: What are they, what are their objectives and what does this imply for poverty-oriented policies?

Labour markets perform two basic functions. They allocate labour among various sectors, occupations and jobs; and they help establish levels of remuneration, thus distributing income to labour force participants. Labour market policies attempt to influence this allocation of labour and its remuneration by affecting the supply of and demand for labour and their interaction. Active labour market policies of the ILO type have four main objectives as indicated in ILO [1993].

> **Efficiency**, *meaning maximum returns* to human resources, maximum output and maximum income — corresponding to economists' criterion for judging the allocation function of labour markets;

> **Equity**, *meaning equality of opportunity for all in access to jobs and training*, equal treatment at work, and equal pay for work of equal value — a concept which contributes to a more equitable distribution of income;

> **Growth**, meaning that labour market operations today should *contribute* to, and not impede, *higher productivity*, income, and improved employment *in the future*;

> **Social justice,** meaning that since labour market outcomes may have positive or negative impacts upon workers' welfare, *society should under certain circumstances act to minimize negative outcomes and redress their harm when they occur*.

It should be noted that the above four objectives are significantly broader in scope compared to those stated by other institutions. The World Bank seems to be mainly concerned with efficiency aspects of labour market policies, concentrating on removing "barriers" to the efficient functioning of labour markets.[8] The OECD concentrates on efficiency and equity [OECD, 1990] with an increasing emphasis in recent years on removing so-called labour market rigidities. The addition in the ILO objectives of "growth" is especially important for developing countries, as it emphasizes the need to be concerned with encouraging improvements in employment and incomes over the long run as compared to short-run redistributive policies that might stunt economic development in the long run. The addition of a social justice objective is important as societies should be concerned with more than arguments of growth, efficiency and equity. When it comes to assisting less fortunate groups in gaining access to employment and avoiding being excluded, exploited or discriminated against, labour market policies can be justified on moral/social justice

---

[8] "Labour markets are responsible for the efficient allocation of labour among production activities and are a major force shaping the primary distribution of incomes... In many industrialized and developing countries, however, labour markets have been diverted from these roles and have become a tool for protection and redistribution of income" [van Adams, 1992].

grounds, even when they cannot be justified based on economic and, especially, efficiency criteria. As stated in the ILO background paper to this Symposium: "The most powerful argument against poverty is not self-interest, but moral" [ILO, 1993a, p. 53]. This statement is especially cogent when it comes to labour market policies for vulnerable groups, because no matter how much one is concerned with efficiency criteria and cost considerations (which is becoming increasingly necessary due to budgetary constraints), it continues to be necessary and acceptable to justify policies for assisting vulnerable groups on moral grounds and criteria of social justice.

Despite the above discussion on labour market policy objectives, it is important to take into consideration trade-offs and constraints in the real world. For example, it is often argued that labour market regulations and policies aimed at protecting workers (such as requiring notice for dismissal, minimum safety standards and maternity leave) only serve to reduce the number of workers protected by encouraging enterprises to avoid such regulations by resorting to use of casual labour, subcontracting out work and by putting formal sector establishment at a competitive disadvantage. Similarly, minimum wage policy (one objective of which is to help the poor who are in a weak bargaining position) is sometimes attacked as having unacceptably large, negative feedback effects on the employment of the poor by pricing them out of employment. There are, of course, counter-arguments in favour of minimum wages and labour market regulations, when it comes to efficiency. Evidence on whether labour market regulations help or hurt is far from conclusive and requires more research and attention [Freeman, 1992]. The ILO, in particular, should seriously address these issues, as its silence in the present world climate would be tantamount to agreement that labour market efficiency and "flexibility" should always take precedence over other labour market objectives.

ILO also needs to work more on identifying appropriate labour market policies to reach the bulk of the poor who are working outside of the formal labour market (especially in developing countries) where, by definition, many labour market policies and regulations do not apply. This will require a broad interpretation of labour market policies to include, for example, promotion and training for self-employment, small enterprise development, and especially support services for poor women with family responsibilities. It will also require linking labour market policies to social and public support policies (such as provision of social services for poor women, including clinics, crèches, water supply and family planning), economic policies (such as improving access of the poor to credit and improved technology), and local area development initiatives (such as public works to provide employment and infrastructure and assessment of local labour skills).

Two important considerations in poverty-oriented labour market policies for disadvantaged groups which also need to be considered are:

1. The cost-effectiveness and sustainability of policies and programmes.

2. The extent to which policies should concentrate on long-term vulnerability, disadvantage and poverty as compared to short-term vulnerability.

Cost effectiveness and self-sustainability are critically important issues that always deserve serious attention. This is especially true for vulnerable groups, since it is common for projects and programmes for such groups to be small in size and relatively expensive in relation to their benefits. This implies that an important area for improving labour market information is in evaluation studies. While small projects are often justified on the basis that they are demonstration projects (and rightly so when they are), cost-effectiveness and sustainability are critical, because it is just not possible to reach the majority of poor in this manner. Also, one must always be on guard against marginalization of vulnerable groups through small projects which isolate vulnerable groups into traditional and marginal activities. This is a major concern for women and the disabled, and for this reason there has been an increasing emphasis in recent years on mainstreaming.

Poverty-oriented labour market policies for vulnerable groups should be concerned with the length of time people are in poverty and disadvantaged in the labour market. There is a big difference between a vulnerable group which is only temporarily in poverty compared to a vulnerable group that stays poor for long periods of time, perhaps for generations. Migrants sometimes provide an example of the first category, while child labourers and certain ethnic/social groups provide examples of the latter category.

V. Specific vulnerable groups and poverty-oriented labour market policies

The above discussion has been general. It has shown that while poverty is usually conceptualized at the household level, poverty is very much labour market-related as the poor are almost exclusively dependent on their work efforts to obtain income. Certain groups are disadvantaged in the labour market, often finding it difficult to get employment and, once in employment, finding it difficult to obtain work with reasonable remuneration and security, acceptable working conditions, and opportunities for upward mobility. This disadvantage may come from a combination of:

   (i) non-labour market factors (such as lower human capital brought to the labour market due to fewer years of formal education and ill-health; cultural restrictions, stereotyping of jobs and perceived abilities; and other constraining responsibilities, such as housework, child care and care of the elderly;

  (ii) labour market functioning (segmented labour markets and occupational crowding; and possibly higher costs to employers);

 (iii) macro-economic and labour market trends and policies (depressed local labour markets due perhaps to disarmament or globalization of production; depressed macro-economic conditions creating longer-term unemployed; wars causing refugees and international migration).

For this reason, it is useful to divide policy options into the following groups. Non-labour market policies which are mainly concerned with:

   (i) education, ill health and disability prior to labour force entry, all of which affect human capital formation;

  (ii) advocacy to help sensitize workers, governments and employers about the importance of the problem and to help in eliminating discrimination and bias based on myths, misconceptions and unacceptable cultural biases;

 (iii) non-economic facilitating policies (such as community child care facilities, family planning and provision of water source near home) to help vulnerable groups cope with non-labour market responsibilities of child care and housework and enable them to be better integrated into the labour market;

 (iv) economic facilitating policies to help those wanting to be self-employed or to own a small business to have a more favourable regulatory and licensing environment as well as to enjoy equal access to complementary inputs, such as credit and new technologies.

Appropriate labour market policies include:

   (i) training and retraining to build up human capital and marketable skills, including basic literacy in countries where this is necessary;

entrepreneurial training in the basics of how to operate a business and training in non-traditional occupations for particular vulnerable groups so that they can become integrated into the labour market;

(ii) wage policies, particularly statutory minimum wages, in countries with sizeable formal sectors;

(iii) labour market policies concerned with affirmative action in order to ensure that vulnerable groups receive job placements;

(iv) direct job creation, usually in public works projects, which could include a food for work element directed towards the poor;

(v) unemployment compensation;

(vi) wage and other related subsidies for employers, when necessary, to compensate for the supposedly higher cost of employing workers from vulnerable groups;

(vii) labour market information for better targeting and planning.

1. Child labour

The abolition of child labour is a core concern of ILO standard setting.[9] A minimum age standard is one of the earliest (Convention 5 of 1919, which relates to child labour in industrial work) and most common type of ILO Conventions (Nos. 5, 10, 32, 59, 60, 123 and 138 all relate to minimum age). In recent years, ILO action on child labour has been intensified due to the Interdepartmental Programme on the Elimination of Child Labour and the International Programme on the Elimination of Child Labour (IPEC).

Child labour is a seemingly easy to understand concept that is often misunderstood when considering its abolition.[10] The internationally

---

[9] This section is concerned with child labour in developing countries. It is important to note that, contrary to popular belief, child labour is not confined to developing countries. The 1992 ILO World Labour Report, for example, mentions that there are over 100,000 child labourers in Spain and the USA and 10,000 in the city of Naples, Italy. A report by the United States Department of Labor and the Mexican Secretariat of Labour and Social Welfare [1992] reports that the United States has labour force participation rates of 8.2 and 16.7 per cent for 14- and 15-year-olds, implying 6.6 million such workers in 1990.

[10] The abolition of child labour serves a purpose quite different from almost all other active labour policies, which are concerned with increasing integration into the world of work. Child labour laws and international standards are concerned with doing the exact opposite — eliminating prospective workers from the labour force. (Encouraging early retirement is another exception.)

accepted definition of "work", i.e. labour force activity, encompasses all "economic" activities which contribute to national income as defined by the United Nations System of National Accounts (SNA). This is a broad definition which includes wage employment, employment in own-business, some unpaid family work, and subsistence-oriented agricultural work. This definition excludes housework and child care because they are not considered to be "economic", in spite of their great value to family survival (see Goldschmidt-Clermont [1990] where a review of 40 studies from developing countries indicates that the value of unpaid household work is equivalent to between 25 and 50 per cent of measured GDP).

The main concern of the ILO and poverty-oriented labour market policies for the abolition of child labour, however, should not be focused on child work per se but on certain forms of work done by children. A useful distinction can be made between "child labour" and "child work". Child labour is concerned with certain types of unacceptable work — work in industries and occupations that are hazardous and/or exploitative (e.g. mines, glassworks, matches/fireworks, prostitution, scavenging); work done by especially young children (e.g. less than 12 years old)[11] that precludes schooling; and work done in bonded relationships that is akin to slavery with all its exploitative and moral aspects. Child work would then logically consist of all other labour force activity.[12] This distinction between child labour and child work is consistent with the discussion in the

---

[11] Sometimes there is confusion regarding the minimum age which should be used to define child labour or child work. Normally this is set at not less than 15 years (based on a reference to the age of primary school completion) although ILO Convention 138 allows for a lower minimum age (14 years in general and 12 years for light work) in the case of countries whose economies and educational facilities are not sufficiently developed. There is also a minimum age of 18 years (with possibility of 16 years under certain conditions) for any type of employment or work which is likely to jeopardize the health, safety or morals of young persons.

[12] It would make sense to extend the distinction between child labour and child work to include the non-labour force activities of housework and child care. Not only do children spend considerable amounts of time in these activities, but their positive and negative (what might be called "labour" and "work") aspects are very much gender-related. Young girls from about 7 to 14 years of age are known to spend much more time on these activities as compared to young boys. Indeed, young girls in developing countries are often responsible for the care of infants and siblings less than the age of five years. In poor households, especially, girls are often the main care-givers because their mothers need to earn money for family survival. Thus, household work and child care could be considered to be child labour when it prevents girls from attending school and/or gaining useful market and income-related skills. This, unfortunately, is the situation in many poor households in many developing countries.

previous section, which emphasized the need to identify subgroups for targeting.

Although minimum age laws are based to a large extent on moral and social justice arguments — childhood is a special "period of life which should be consecrated not to work but to education and development" [ILO, 1992b] and the employment of children is often seen as an affront to human dignity — these are not the only arguments which can be used to justify the abolition of child labour. Efficiency and growth are also active labour market policy objectives, which can also be promoted by the elimination of child labour, especially when one considers a longer time perspective. By engaging in child labour at an early age, children are burdened for the rest of their lives. They forego the acquisition of education and skills that would make them more productive workers in adult life; and they subject themselves to unhealthy conditions and possible disability, and also probably stunt their social and mental development. These effects have long-term negative consequences on labour productivity. In short, child labour exerts a negative effect in the long run on economic growth and labour market efficiency. It can also be argued that child labour reduces economic growth in another manner — by providing a crutch to employers, thereby slowing innovation and investment as employers learn to rely on a cheap and exploitable source of labour. Finally, the abolition of child labour can be justified based on the equity objective. The presence of child labour increases the likelihood that all workers face more exploitative working conditions and lower wages as the supply of child labour reduces the bargaining position of all workers (particularly poor unskilled adult workers with few other work opportunities).

In the light of arguments made above, we may ask why child labour continues to exist. The answer indicates why child labour must be of central concern in a poverty-oriented labour market policy. Child labour is a consequence (as well as a cause) of poverty. Children from the poorest households are the most likely to be child labourers at an early age and such families often see child labour as absolutely necessary for survival. This helps to create a series of vicious poverty cycles and traps. There is the life cycle poverty trap for the child, as discussed above. There is the vicious cycle whereby child labour encourages higher fertility by increasing the value of children which, in turn, helps to reinforce family poverty. There is the inter-generational vicious cycle whereby child labourers become more likely to have large families with low incomes when they become adults,[13] and thus more likely to have their own children work as child labourers.

So what should be done to abolish child labour within a poverty-oriented labour market policy approach? Put bluntly, if child labour is poverty-induced, is it possible or even reasonable to deny children the "right to work", as this might increase or intensify poverty for these children and their families? Long-run oriented arguments as discussed above are not always felt to be relevant by households at or below the poverty line as they are mainly concerned with survival today. In fact, enforcement of minimum age legislation, in relatively visible, formal sector occupations and sectors, could conceivably make the poverty situation worse; it is possible that the child labourers being "saved" may simply shift to less lucrative and more exploitative occupations.[14] In a sense then, child labour policy is seemingly poised between a rock and a hard place. Child labour may be seen as wrong both morally and economically from the society's point of view, but often seen as necessary by the family for its survival.

A reasonable approach to this dilemma consists of the following, as developed in the recent ILO policy statement "Towards the abolition of child labour: ILO policy and its implications for technical co-operation activities" [ILO, 1993b], which draws on the flexibility built into Convention 138. It recognizes that while "the fundamental objective of the ILO in this matter is the elimination of child labour... the complete abolition of child labour will take a long time in view of the deep-seated causes of such work". In this light, the policy statement suggests concentrating efforts on measures to:

1. Stop urgently intolerable forms of child labour (in hazardous work and use of very young children).

2. Change attitudes regarding the social acceptability of child labour (through mobilizing and sensitizing public opinion and pressure groups).

---

[13] Other important determinants of fertility include education (negative) and infant/child mortality (positive), both of which are likely to cause child labourers to have high fertility when they become adults.

[14] It has been reported in the media, for example, that children working in the garment industry in Bangladesh were laid off *en masse* because of adverse publicity which the industry was receiving. Reports of the consequences of this action are disheartening — many of the children who were laid off are reported to have taken up worse forms of work, such as prostitution, scavenging and street work.

3.   Attack the root causes of child labour (by improving the economic situation of the poor).

As recognized in the ILO policy statement, eliminating even extreme and unacceptable forms of child labour will take time in some countries — so that a transition period is unavoidable — and during this period it is acceptable to be concerned with helping the working child. This is not to be taken as condoning and accepting child labour — as activists sometimes complain — as long as efforts are framed within an overall goal of abolishing child labour.[15]

This concern for the welfare of child labourers is essential if the ILO is to be credible, as working children are extremely vulnerable to exploitation and health and moral hazards, and many times are without any family support. Provision of shelters and organizing street children are facilitating and labour market programmes to be recommended. Also to be recommended are programmes which would allow children to effectively combine training and work, perhaps at the workplace — although one would have to be very careful that such programmes did not degenerate into exploitative "apprenticeships".

In making efforts to stop intolerable forms of child labour, it is also necessary to have credible programmes to help replace both supply and demand reasons for child labour. Regarding the supply side, it is necessary to: (i) raise income levels among the poor so that they can "afford" to stop having their children work as child labourers; (ii) have credible alternative options (in the opinion of the poor family) for the child's time. The first of these requirements implies the need for poverty-oriented economic development, but this is hardly a new recommendation. What could be "new" would be to target areas and households where child labour is common. This would be a feasible approach in countries where child labour is clustered by village, city, slum neighbourhood or region, as is the case in parts of India and Nepal according to the author's own experience.

The second point is usually taken to imply the need to establish local schools and make primary education compulsory: if children go to school, they cannot be child labourers. This argument draws on the historical experience of currently developed countries and seemingly ironclad logic. The major problem with the solution of compulsory education is that the education system is not always credible to poor people and so they do not

---

[15] This being said, certain forms of child labour cannot be accepted, even in the short-run. This would apply to bonded labour and especially hazardous work (although on this latter point it is necessary to be sure that a particular type of work is in fact hazardous).

always send their children to school — even when it is available at a short distance from home. Poor families do not always see education as relevant or useful. Curricula are often seen as too "academic" and the quality of the instruction as poor. Thus, while compulsory education is important for economic development and elimination of child labour in the long run, it is not an immediate panacea, and authorities should be working to improve the availability and relevance of schooling for poor families.

The demand for child labour, on the other hand, has received very little attention among either researchers or policy-makers. Employers are generally seen by activists in demonic terms as exploiters of children and as a major obstacle to enforcement of minimum age laws. Employers, of course, do not see themselves this way. In fact, they often believe that they are helping children and their families to survive by providing employment and income to children.

It is important not to neglect the role of employers, especially in a tripartite organization such as the ILO. Practical reality alone dictates that eliminating child labour would be easier if it were possible to work with employers and employers' groups. In addition, historical experience indicates that employers with something to gain from the elimination of child labour (perhaps because they are using a more productive process requiring more capital investment) have been among the most influential in reducing and eliminating the use of child labour.

With the above in mind, the author has worked with Indian colleagues at the Centre for Operations Research and Training (CORT), with Deborah Levison (University of Minnesota), and with ILO's Programmes on Child Labour — IPEC (International Programme on the Elimination of Child Labour) and the Interdepartmental Programme on Child Labour — to investigate the economies of eliminating child labour in two "prohibited" and hazardous industries in India, carpet-weaving and glass bangles (bracelets). The following types of questions are being investigated: why are children hired (e.g. do children have irreplaceable skills — the so-called "nimble fingers" arguments? Are children less expensive and/or more productive)? How many (and what percentage) of workers are children in these industries? What are the working conditions; what could be done to help employers replace children with adults? What would be the cost and sales implications for the industry if child labour were eliminated? Last but not least (pointedly), would the industry survive without child labour?

Preliminary results from these Indian studies provide interesting and useful insights. For advocacy purposes with governments and employers, results from the study of the glass bangles industry indicate that children do not provide irreplaceable skills; at the same time the use of child labour has virtually no effect on the cost of production as all workers are paid on a piece-rate basis. In the carpet industry, children do not appear to have irreplaceable skills as is commonly believed, but they do provide a cost advantage to some employers. For development strategy and targeting purposes, it is important to note that the supply of child labour appears to be clustered in both industries regarding area of origin, and so amenable to local area programme interventions targeted on the children and their families. For international agencies, it is important to note that there is fierce international competition in the hand-knotted carpet industry (the largest exporters being India, China, Pakistan, Iran and Nepal) which means that international and/or regional initiatives are required.[16] The above discussion indicates that there is great scope for improved labour market information, analysis and research on child labour. For example, there is a need to understand better the health hazards under which child labourers work, in order to target programme efforts towards those situations where working conditions are especially hazardous.[17] Such studies should investigate psychological (mental and emotional) development as well as physical problems, as the monotonous and repetitive work often done by children might have a bigger negative effect on the former than the latter.

There is a need for more and better studies on the economics of eliminating child labour in different types of hazardous industries, similar to the studies the author is currently undertaking for carpets and glass bangles in India. There are undoubtedly a number of different models on how child labour is inserted in an industry (depending on the organization of production and sales, technology options and labour skills required). There are also undoubtedly important country-specific differences for the same industry and there is clearly much to be gained by additional studies to enhance advocacy and action for all three of ILO's constituents.

---

[16] It would not make sense for international agencies, or be acceptable to countries, to reduce child labour in one country if it simply meant that exports and child labour were thereby increased in another country. There is the danger that this could happen in the carpet industry if a regional or international approach is not taken.

[17] Such studies are required because the effects of poor working conditions are likely to be quite different for children and adults; there may also be important interactions between undernourishment, physical underdevelopment and poor working conditions. Surprisingly, there are few good studies on the health hazards faced by child labourers. In situations of extreme poverty, it is even conceivable that the health of child labourers could be improved as the negative consequences of working could be counterbalanced by what can be purchased by the income earned.

There is a need for evaluation and studies on the cost-effectiveness of programmes. Such evaluations should include tracer studies and follow-up studies to assess working conditions and determine what has happened to the children and enterprises.

There is a need to study the link between family size (fertility) and child labour and, in particular, to discover whether or not high fertility causes child labour. In other words, are poor families with many children more likely to have their children work as labourers as compared to poor families with few children?

Better measurement of the numbers of children found in different industries, occupations, cities and regions is needed and for this it would be important to distinguish between different types of child labour. For example, in terms of working hours and attendance at school; work relationships with employers where children are not self-employed or are unpaid family workers; hazardousness of working conditions; current age and age when starting working; occupation; skills required; and specific industrial sector. With such information, policy-makers would be able better to identify and target the most needy and largest groups of child labourers, as the most visible forms of child labour should not necessarily be the focus of attention.

Studies are needed of local areas where child labour is concentrated, in order to devise appropriate policies and programmes for assisting affected families, ethnic groups and regions so as to reduce the need for, and supply of, child labour.

2. Disabled workers

There is considerable misinformation about disability among both lay persons and policy-makers. A generally-held impression is that there are relatively small numbers of persons who are incapacitated by, for example, loss of sight, hearing or limb, and that these persons require quite specialized and expensive treatment and/or other assistance, in order to enable them to become productive members of the labour force.

This impression is incorrect. First of all, disability is very common. Data from developed countries indicate that approximately 10 per cent of the working age population has a disability [OECD, 1992]. A 1987 national survey of 1.25 million households in China indicates that 18 per cent of all households have at least one disabled person [Chamie, 1989]. Data from transition economies in Eastern and Central Europe indicate similar disability rates to those prevailing in Western Europe [ILO, CEET, 1993].[18]

A distinction can be usefully made between "impairment", "disability" and "handicap". *Impairment* is defined by the World Health Organisation as "any loss or abnormality of psychological, physiological or anatomical structure or function." This is a medical definition, with estimates of impairment often based on survey questions about blindness, deafness, paralysis or loss of limb, mutism and mental retardation, etc.

Disability is defined by the WHO as a "restriction or lack (resulting from an impairment) of ability to perform an activity in the manner or within the range considered normal for a human being." Typical survey questions to measure disability usually enquire about difficulty or inability to perform certain activities as regards mobility, agility, seeing, hearing, speaking, mental retardation and psychological problems.

Handicap is defined by WHO as a "disadvantage for a given individual resulting from an impairment or disability that limits or prevents the fulfilment of a role that is normal (depending on age, sex and social and cultural factors) for that individual". Thus, the concept of disadvantaged used in this chapter is equivalent to this definition of handicap. It is also consistent with the definition of "disabled person" used in ILO Convention 159 on Vocation Rehabilitation and Employment (Disabled Persons): "the term disabled person means an individual whose prospects of securing, retaining and advancing in suitable employment are subsequently reduced as a result of a duly recognized physical or mental impairment" [ILO, 1983].

The emphasis in this chapter is on the labour market disadvantages faced by disabled persons and the fact that this disadvantage is itself determined/defined by societal, cultural and development level factors. This perspective stresses what disabled persons can do (with perhaps some assistance such as in training and transport) and not what they cannot do. There are countless examples of disabled persons who have jobs and are productive members of society, ranging from Franklin Roosevelt and

---

[18] There are major problems with the accuracy of available data on disability due to the use of different definitions (e.g. medical-oriented impairment type definitions compared to functional disability type definitions), different questionnaire formats (e.g. use of one general keyword type question compared to use of a series of detailed questions describing different types of disability), different samples (e.g. working age population compared to total population) [United Nations, 1990]. Indeed, the United Nations Statistical Compendium [1990] reports a range of estimated disability rates from 0.2 per cent (Peru) to 20.9 per cent (Austria) partly because of these problems.

Steven Hawking, to blind computer programmers and to mentally handi-capped persons working in McDonald's.

In contrast, there is an unfortunate tendency in many countries to treat disability as a medical condition only and thus to emphasize what disabled persons cannot do. In the transition economies in Eastern and Central Europe and the former Soviet Union, this was bureaucratized into three levels of disability based on medical assessments of the percentage of reduced capacity of a disabled person. This approach stigmatizes disabled persons and makes employers more reluctant to hire them.

There are important links between disability and poverty; disabled persons are poorer on average — although, surprisingly, there is relatively little empirical evidence on this. The linkage is bi-directional. Poverty causes disability in so far as certain diseases (such as polio, leprosy and measles) and accidents (such as burns) are much more common among the poor, especially in developing countries. In India, for example, polio accounts for 40 per cent of limb deformity and 30 per cent of paralysis, while leprosy accounts for approximately another 7 per cent of limb deformity [United Nations, 1990]. Persons who become disabled when young or have some degree of mental retardation are much less likely to receive adequate education, especially if they are from a poor household. Disability also causes poverty for individuals and families, unless adequate income transfers or other assistance is received by them from the state (as occurs in some industrialized countries), due to reduced working capacity and increased discrimination.

This being said, the disabled are a very heterogeneous group. While they are poorer on average, there is a wide range in their situations; some are poor, some are middle-class and some are well-to-do. It is very important to keep this heterogeneity in mind, in order to avoid stereotyping and the labelling of disabled persons, as well as to devise appropriately targeted policies.

Active labour market policies for disabled persons can be justified by all four of ILO's labour market objectives. Keeping in mind that disabled persons comprise approximately 10 per cent of the working age population, it is clear that increased labour market efficiency and economic growth would result from a more active participation of disabled persons in a non-discriminatory labour market environment. The underutilization (e.g. low activity rates) and inefficient use (e.g. concentration in low-wage, low-skill occupations) of the disabled reduces labour market efficiency and economic growth. Despite these arguments, equity and social justice objectives are the main justifications of active labour market policies for the disabled. Due to misinformation, unfounded stereotypes and discrimination in the labour market, disabled persons do not have an equal chance of finding employment and are particularly disadvantaged in regard to advancement and higher quality jobs. In addition to these prejudices, disabled persons often are disadvantaged in the labour market due to factors affecting productivity, such as lower education, less experience and physical or mental restrictions. Therefore, the social justice objective is important. For the disabled, this often means "levelling" the playing field by providing them with special education when young or vocational training when adults; support services and/or facilities for transport, housework and medical care; assistance in starting a business; and designing specific labour market laws/regulations/policies to promote their employment.

The labour market and income situation of the disabled varies greatly across industrialized (OECD) countries, transition economy countries and developing countries. The commitment of governments toward assisting the disabled also varies greatly across these three types of countries. OECD governments commit large amounts of resources to labour market programmes for the disabled, ranging up to 0.90 per cent of GDP in Sweden in 1992 [OECD, 1993]. As OECD governments are responsible for providing large social/income transfers to the disabled they are increasingly interested in activating disabled persons, via active labour market policies (including equal rights and anti-discrimination laws as in Australia, Canada and the United States; quotas systems as in France and Germany; wage subsidy systems in Sweden; and employment service training, counselling and placement).

Transition economies are now in crisis and the situation of the disabled is particularly bad. Under the old regime, the disabled were integrated into the labour market. Using sheltered workshops and quota systems, disabled persons found employment (in a highly segregated manner). With the transition to a market economy, and the new concern for costs and profits, enterprises are less interested in keeping disabled workers. Indeed, employers often prefer to pay a fine for not employing their quota of disabled workers (which is often quite low; it is for example 2,500 forints per year, or US$26, in Hungary). As a result, the disabled persons who continue to find employment in this region are increasingly concentrated in sheltered workshops [ILO-CEET, 1993]. Furthermore, those on disability pension have become pauperized due to high inflation rates. This is a desperate poverty situation that requires short-run solutions to provide sufficient income support and/or employment as well as long-term labour market solutions.

In developing countries, disability policies and programmes do not appear to be high on the policy agenda, with the possible exception of disabled war veterans (although information here is very incomplete). The general assumptions seem to be that:

1. The disabled are generally taken care of by their families and so are not a particularly pressing poverty concern.

2. In the light of the large numbers of able-bodied persons who are unemployed or underemployed, it is more effective to spend scarce government resources on able bodied people.

3. Most policies and programmes for disabled workers would not be effective, in any case, because of large informal sectors.

These assumptions made for developing countries are not always correct. First, with modernization and urbanization, the extended family system is weakening in the developing world and thus many weaker members of society, such as older persons (and also disabled persons) can no longer take for granted that they will be taken care of by family members [Nugent & Anker, 1990]. Secondly, social justice and concern for weaker members of society dictate that governments should be concerned about helping disabled persons in the labour market. Thirdly, as discussed below, there may be cost-effective policy and programme options for the disabled, despite the informal nature of labour markets in many developing countries.

Rather than treating each of the three types of countries (industrialized, transition, developing) separately, the following discussion stresses commonalities in policy objectives, policy options and future research priorities, while also noting differences. The main emphasis should be on *integrating* disabled persons into the labour market. Efforts should be directed toward enabling disabled workers to obtain jobs where they work alongside non-disabled workers, rather than emphasizing separate enterprises/workshops (except for severely disabled persons). This implies putting an emphasis on enabling policies and programmes, such as training to enhance skill levels and, where it can be afforded, assistance in transportation and household tasks. In industrialized countries, wage subsidies or other assistance to employers to compensate for higher costs associated with disabled workers would make sense, although it is important to guard against deadweight costs.

In transition economies and developing countries, this also implies providing an enabling atmosphere for self-employment, including training, in bookkeeping and marketing, etc.; assistance in gaining access to credit (perhaps by guaranteeing, or subsidizing, small business loans as done in a recent, successful ILO project in Kenya); provision of tax advantages in more industrialized countries and reducing regulatory barriers in developing countries; and establishing hot lines for providing advice and assistance at short notice when major difficulties arise.

This approach also implies a need to emphasize the types of work done by disabled workers. Despite a general lack of data on types of jobs held by disabled workers, even in industrialized countries, there is agreement that disabled workers are concentrated in a small range of low-skill, dead-end jobs. This segregation and marginalizing of disabled workers should be at least as much a concern to policy-makers as finding employment for disabled persons.

In terms of research priorities, several suggestions are made below. We need to learn more about the policy, programme commitments and interests of governments in developing countries. How important/unimportant are disability issues; what programmes and projects are being implemented and how much is being spent on them? Are there special programmes for disabled war veterans?

We need to learn more about labour force participation of disabled persons and their types of occupations and pay received. Whenever possible such information should be linked to the income/poverty situation of the disabled person's household. The chief concern should be on monitoring changes over time. Such information would make it easier to demonstrate the magnitude of the disability problem (e.g. the extent to which disabled are in poverty; their number, occupations and income received) and to target appropriate assistance better suited to those in need.

Special attention should be paid to investigating the frequency with which disabled persons are in positions of authority and in occupations with progressive career paths involving possible promotion. Attention should also be given to examining the extent to which disabled persons are concentrated in a small range of low-level, dead-end occupations, and identifying what are non-traditional jobs for disabled persons. In such investigations, whenever possible, a dynamic, longitudinal perspective should be used to observe labour mobility and the changing situation over time.

Government policies regarding their hiring and promotion practices should be reviewed, as governments could provide considerable employment for disabled persons and could also demonstrate their commitment to private enterprises with respect to such employment.

There is a need to evaluate objectively the cost-effectiveness of programmes for the disabled (e.g. wage subsidies, sheltered workshops, redesigned workshops, training, etc.). At a time of restricted government budgets and with the desire to integrate disabled persons into the mainstream of the labour market, it is important that policy-makers receive feedback on the effectiveness of projects and programmes, and to learn from successes and failures. The same need for evaluation would apply to employment services offices, which are often responsible for identifying jobs, training and counselling. How well are they doing such work? These evaluations of programmes and employment services should also include tracer surveys of disabled persons who have been assisted.

As successful disability programmes and policies will increasingly depend on placement of disabled workers in private sector enterprises, it is important to understand the possibilities for such placement as seen from the employers' point of view. In the process, it would be worthwhile to separate out discriminatory behaviour, which is based on misinformation and stereotyping, from legitimate concerns of employers regarding higher costs and lower productivity. Based on such an understanding, policy-makers would be better positioned to sensitize and work with employers. This implies the usefulness of undertaking industry-specific studies, including enterprise surveys and in-depth discussions with employers, which could also involve investigating, analysing and reporting on those cases where significant numbers of disabled persons were successfully employed and were as productive as other workers.

3. Women

Although women are not a minority group (like child labourers and disabled persons) and are even more heterogeneous with respect to poverty than these other groups, women should still be considered as a disadvantaged and vulnerable group. Women, on average, earn less than men and tend to be concentrated in a reduced set of relatively low wage, dead-end types of jobs and occupations [Anker & Hein, 1986]. Female-dominated occupations also tend to be undervalued in terms of pay compared to male-dominated occupations [Gunderson, 1994].

There are important aspects of women's position in society and the labour market that distinguish women from men and cause women to be disadvantaged in the labour market, and many of them to be vulnerable. First, women are responsible in all societies for household work and the bearing and caring of children, and there is evidence that the health and survival of children is strongly related to the mother's education, knowledge and experience. This helps to explain, for example, the continued improvements in life expectancy in Africa in recent years, despite an economic crisis [World Bank, 1993].[19] Household and child care responsibilities result in the so-called double burden for women workers which affects labour supply and labour demand.[20] Some women withdraw from the labour force when they become married or have young children. Many women — especially poor women, who are often household heads, and cannot afford to be out of the labour force — must frequently engage in types of work compatible with their family responsibilities, such as work which is flexible in terms of hours and close to home and children.

Secondly, women are often discriminated against with regard to human capital acquisition. This occurs both within the household, in terms of the allocation of resources, e.g. girls receiving less education than boys and females of all ages receiving less food and health care [Haddad & Kaubur, 1990; Anker et al., 1989].[21] Discrimination also occurs in the labour market (which is taken up below). Thirdly, there are a number of very damaging misconceptions and stereotypes regarding women and their need for income. It is assumed too often that women are secondary earners whose income is supplementary in nature ("pocket money"), and the women are therefore not as much in need of a job as the men. This view flies in face of the fact that many of the world's households are headed by a woman; and also ignores the truth that most poor households require the income of several household members for their survival. Fourthly, many occupations are thought to be suitable (and so are basically reserved) only for men or only for women. The high degree to which there is occupational stereotyping in the world can be illustrated by data taken from a study on occupational segregation in which the present author and Jim Windell are currently engaged.

---

[19] There is, on the other hand, controversy about whether or not women's labour force activity improves or hurts their children's health and survival, especially among poorer households. The traditionalist view is that women's labour force activity has a negative effect on children's health and survival as it generally causes the mother to be separated from her child and so reduces her personal time and care inputs to the child. A counter-argument adhered to by many is that female labour force activity improves the child's health and survival, because of increased family income to buy food and medical services, the greater influence and autonomy within the family which a woman supposedly gains because of her contribution to family income, and greater access to information and modern behaviour which work often brings [Khan et al., 1992]. In all probability, the relative importance of these factors varies by household income level and age of the child.

[20] The so-called triple burden (work, child care, care of the elderly) has now become important in many countries.

[21] For example, in a study of the carpet industry in rural India in which the author is currently engaged, over 90 per cent of male loom owners' wives had never attended school.

Table 1: Selected cross-national examples of typically female-dominant or female-concentrated occupations

Occupation	Country and percentage of women in comparable occupational group				
	China 1980	Luxembourg 1991	Japan 1991	Norway 1990	Malaysia 1980
Nurses	94.73	55.22	96.74	92.25	72.05[1]
Hairdressers, barbers, beauticians and related workers	n/a	77.69	69.11	90.00	60.09
Stenographers, typists, etc.	86.34	91.93	93.32[1]	82.00	90.90
Tailors, dressmakers, sewers, upholsterers, etc.	79.84[1]	89.29	80.39	53.00 (x)	79.89
Teachers (all levels)	39.07 (x)	52.62 (x)	43.42 (x)	48.38 (x)	45.65
Maids and related housekeeping services workers	n/a	99.15	97.38	84.00	93.86
Bookkeepers, cashiers and related workers	n/a	56.35	75.63[1]	75.25	49.38
Salespersons, shop assistants, etc.	56.89	79.30	60.52	66.33 (x)	30.33 (x)
Cooks, waiters, bartenders, etc.	44.96[1] (x)	52.94 (x)	61.88	79.00	45.89

Notes: [1] Classification of occupational group only roughly comparable with standard ISCO-68 classification.

    (x) denotes an occupation which is neither female-dominant or -concentrated.

    For all countries n/a means no comparable occupation was available for comparison.

    Female-dominated occupations defined as 80 per cent or more female.

    Female-concentrated occupations defined as greater than or equal to 1.5 * mean per cent female in labour force.

    Per cent of labour force which is female: Luxembourg 35.89 per cent, Norway 47.14 per cent, Japan 39.2 per cent, China 35.7 per cent, Malaysia 28.2 per cent.

Source: Preliminary data from Anker and Windell (forthcoming).

Table 2: Selected cross-national examples of typically male-dominant occupations

Occupation	Country and percentage of men in comparable occupational group					
	China 1980	Luxembourg 1991	Japan 1991	Norway 1990	Malaysia 1980	
Architects, engineers and related technicans	75.27 (x)	94.46	97.40	78.43 (x)	92.17	
Legislative officials and government administrators	93.63	93.63	87.44	59.00 (x)	80.28	
Managers	91.05	87.57	90.78	90.00	93.22	
Sales supervisors and buyers	82.21	85.57	76.59 (x)	73.00 (x)	84.43	
Protective service workers	93.74	96.82	97.16	81.00	97.58	
Production supervisors and general foremen	n/a	98.82	n/a	n/a	88.22	
Blacksmiths, toolmakers, etc.	89.26	98.19	91.33	96.25	88.35	
Bricklayers, carpenters and other construction workers	95.35	99.32	95.66	97.83	94.53	

Notes: n/a means no comparable occupation was available for comparison.
(x) denotes a non-male-dominant occupation.
Male-dominated occupations are defined as greater than or equal to 80 per cent male.

Source: Preliminary data from Anker and Windell (forthcoming).

Tables 1 and 2 present data from two European and three Asian countries on rates of feminization for 17 occupations, which are frequently considered to be appropriate for either men or women. There is a high degree of consistency, with occupations tending to be predominately male or female, although there are also some exceptions. Making this situation especially difficult for women workers is the fact that they have a much more restricted set of occupations as compared to men.

This phenomenon is shown in Tables 3a and 3b for six Asian countries. Whereas 40 to 50 per cent of male workers are in male-dominated occupations (defined as those employing at least 80 per cent men) and such occupations comprise about 40 per cent of all occupations for which data was obtained, female-dominated occupations comprised only about 3 per cent of all occupations and only about 10 to 15 per cent of women workers were in such occupations. In addition, female-dominated occupations tend to be relatively low paid [Barbezat, 1993]. Rationalizations used to exclude women workers from male-dominated jobs include such explanations as their supposed lack of muscular strength, inability to supervise, inability to work late, and possible harassment by male co-workers; explanations in favour of hiring women workers for female-dominated jobs include docility, caring nature, appearance, household-related skills and low reservation wage. Employers in the formal sector also often see women workers as being more costly, on average, due to higher turnover, more work absences, greater tardiness and maternity leave. Although the cost factors have some validity, many assumptions about women workers are often incorrect.[22]

Labour market policies for women are usually justified with reference to efficiency and, even more so, to equity objectives. Women should have the same opportunities as men to gain employment, to be promoted, to freely choose their occupation, and to receive pay commensurate with the value of their work. In meeting these equity objectives, there would be an improvement in labour market efficiency and economic growth, as the abilities of women are more effectively utilized.

---

[22] In a series of developing country studies using enterprise and worker surveys in Cyprus, Ghana, India, Nigeria and Sri Lanka, it was found that the perception of employers of greater absenteeism and labour turnover among women workers (due largely to maternity and family responsibilities) was not quite borne out by the data. Women had higher turnover rates due to marriage, childbirth and child care whereas men had higher rates due to voluntary resignation and drinking; these causes were roughly of the same magnitude [Anker & Hein, 1985]. Enterprise surveys of the recent situation in the transition economies of Bulgaria and Hungary (Standing et al., 1993) found considerable gender bias among employers.

Table 3a: Summary of female-dominated occupations,¹ Asia (all samples exclude agricultural workers)

Country	Year	% labour force female	Total number of occupations	Number of female-dominated occupations	% employment share of female-dominated occupations in total labour force	% female labour force in female-dominated occupations	% male labour force in female-dominated occupations
China	1980	35.7	277	14	5.7	15.0	0.60
Hong Kong	1991	37.9	72	3	5.9	14.6	0.60
Japan	1990	39.2	265	4	7.3	16.6	1.20
India	1981	12.1	425	3	0.4	2.9	0.04
S. Korea	1989	34.5	44	1	5.3	12.7	1.30
Malaysia	1980	28.3	76	2	3.0	9.8	0.30

Note: ¹ A female-dominated occupation consists of 80 per cent or more females.

Source: Preliminary data from Anker and Windell (forthcoming).

Table 3b: Summary of male-dominated occupations,[1] Asia (all samples exclude agricultural workers)

Country	Year	% labour force male	Total number of occupations	Number of male-dominated occupations	% employment share of male-dominated occupations in total labour force	% male labour force in male-dominated occupations	% female labour force in male-dominated occupations
China	1980	64.3	277	77	30.5	43.4	7.3
Hong Kong	1991	62.1	72	28	28.5	42.5	5.5
Japan	1990	60.8	265	119	35.3	54.1	6.0
India	1981	87.9	425	378	81.02	86.24	43.25
S. Korea	1989	65.5	44	18	26.7	38.5	4.4
Malaysia	1980	71.7	76	36	42.0	55.8	4.0

Note: [1] A male-dominated occupation consists of 80 per cent or more males.
Source: Preliminary data from Anker and Windell (forthcoming).

The types of labour market policies required for helping poor women differ somewhat between industrialized countries, transition economies and developing countries, depending on the extent to which labour market regulations and policies can be effectively implemented, which in turn depends very much on the relative size of formal sector employment. In industrialized countries, for example, minimum wages can be an effective labour market instrument for helping poor women and have been recommended as such by a network of experts reporting to the Commission of the European Communities [Rubery & Fagan, 1993]. Comparable worth policies can be effective in raising wages of low-paying occupations which have been unfairly undervalued, although to date these policies have not been widely applied [Gunderson, 1994]. Affirmative action programmes can be effective in improving women's chances for obtaining new and better-paying jobs and entry into what are now male-dominated occupations. In transition economies, where women have been relatively well integrated into the labour market, it is important to ensure that the creation of a market economy does not result in women workers losing out, as appears to be the case at the present time [Paukert, 1993]. In developing countries, wage differentials for the same work still appear to be sizeable [e.g. Bardham, 1989] and so efforts should be redoubled to eliminate this form of direct discrimination.

All three types of countries, however, have a number of common features with respect to the labour market disadvantage of women and therefore to some extent need similar appropriate labour market policies. First, education, training and development of human capital needs to be stressed. Most societies under-invest in skill development for women as compared to men. This begins with basic education for girls and continues through to vocational training for adult women. Even when women attain similar levels of education there usually remains a gender bias in that women tend to be concentrated in the humanities rather than in the sciences. Labour market policies also need to stress skill development and training in order to increase women's productivity and thus to provide them with an equal chance in the labour market. This would include basic literacy courses where necessary, courses in how to be more effective self-employed businesswomen, and vocational training particularly for non-traditional occupations.

Secondly, it is important to break down labour market segregation by gender in order to improve women's chances in the labour market. This requires a number of common approaches, including skill development (discussed above), and facilitating policies (discussed below) as well as sensitization and the changing of biased, preconceived notions of appropriate roles and abilities of male and female workers. For this, we need to know much more about the extent and patterns of labour market desegregation by gender (as well as for other vulnerable groups). This requires detailed occupational data at the two, three or four digit levels of classification. It is not sufficient to know what proportion of women are working in professional, administrative/managerial, sales, service, clerical, agricultural and production occupations. Indeed, such aggregated occupational data sometimes leads to erroneous conclusions about the degree of occupational segregation [Anker & Windell, forthcoming]. For example, women may be well represented among professionals, yet virtually all professional women may be concentrated in two occupations, teachers and nurses, (and even within these occupations in certain subgroups, such as primary school teachers). We also need to know more about which occupations are changing from being male-dominated to being more gender-mixed occupations in particular countries, and then to learn how and why this has occurred, in order to devise appropriate policies and programmes to encourage such changes. Information is required about the generally negative relationship prevailing between feminization of occupations and income/pay, and how/why this changes, in order to devise appropriate policies and programmes to combat this tendency.

Thirdly, in all countries we need to know more about how effectively various policies and programmes designed to assist poor women are proceeding. In terms of research, this implies impact assessment and cost-effectiveness studies of projects for women; it also requires paying attention to whether or not traditional patterns of labour market inequality such as occupational segregation, are being reinforced or broken down by projects.

Fourthly, more needs to be known about the reasons why employers do or do not hire or promote women. How much bias is there? Is it greater among certain types of employers? How much of the bias is based on myths and discrimination as compared to legitimate cost and productivity concerns? Based on such information, it should be possible to sensitize and educate employers; at least, it would provide a basis for constructive dialogue. In terms of research, this implies the usefulness of enterprise-level surveys and in-depth case studies of employers to understand better the demand side of women's labour market disadvantages.

Fifthly, women workers would benefit from various facilitating policies in the light of their family and household responsibilities. This includes provision of: family planning services (to allow women control over their bodies and to reduce family size); health services and primary health care (to reduce illness and the need for home care); crèches and community facilities for child care (to allow women to work away from home); community infrastructural facilities, such as water taps, electricity and fuel (to help reduce the household burden). This also includes changing laws and regulations that restrict women's ability to run their own businesses, such as having equal access to credit and the right to own property; all too often women do not have the same rights as men, sometimes in law and often in practice. This also includes assisting self-employed women by providing technical advisory services, organizing them as SEWA has done in India and helping them with credit schemes as done by the Grameen Bank in Bangladesh.

Sixthly, women frequently work in informal, casual work relationships, often in exploitative circumstances. This includes self-employment as petty traders in the informal sector as well as various forms of home production in developing countries. It also includes wage employment with casual work contracts and few, if any, employment projections in newly-industrialized countries, as well as part-time employment without social protection in industrializing countries [Standing, 1989]. This includes (in all countries) domestic maids and prostitutes. Research studies focusing on these and other highly exploitative forms of employment should be encouraged.

Another research priority includes studying the link between the earnings of income by women and the welfare of families and children. We need more evidence to convince policy-makers on both:

(i) the extent to which women have more socially positive expenditure patterns regarding overall household welfare and its distribution among household members (e.g. resulting in better health, education, nutrition, clothing);

(ii) the extent to which working and earning increase a woman's influence over household decision-making.

The former will vary greatly by region and country, while the latter is by no means a straightforward conclusion. For example, in a study in rural North India, in which the present author collaborated, approximately one-half of study women earning wages (usually as daily agricultural workers) did not receive their pay, as the employer gave it directly to the husband and, of the other half, which did receive their wages, approximately one-half of them reported that they immediately gave their pay to their husbands (unpublished data).

VI. Summary and conclusions

This chapter has been concerned with labour market policies for vulnerable groups as viewed within a poverty context. It began by noting that since poor, vulnerable groups rely almost exclusively on labour income, labour market policies should play a crucial role in poverty-oriented policy approaches. It went on to discuss how the conceptualization and measurement of poverty are usually based on household income or consumption, whereas labour market policies are concerned with individuals or groups of individuals. It was concluded that poverty-oriented labour market policies should focus on persons from vulnerable groups located in low-wage/low-income segments of the labour market and generally ignore an individual's household income status; it is important to guard against any tendency to treat persons in vulnerable groups as secondary earners who do not need assistance.

It was also concluded that there is a need for the ILO and other organizations to undertake research on labour market indicators that reflect and monitor poverty, perhaps using rapid assessment techniques and approaches. Measures of poverty-related labour market conditions could include unemployment rates and size of the informal sector; wage rates for poor persons, such as statutory minimum wages and wage rates for unskilled workers in agriculture, construction and services (in real terms, adjusted for inflation and perhaps the cost of the most important staple foods); numbers of workers with casual/temporary contracts and holding multiple jobs; and occupational segregation by gender, age, ethnicity and disability, etc.

The discussion identified some important, general labour market issues for future research. For developing countries, it is important to be concerned with labour market policies for the poor who work in the informal sector and so are not covered by labour market regulations or standards. In many developing countries, where considerable economic growth and industrialization has occurred in recent years (e.g. newly-industrializing countries, NICs), there should be considerable scope for extending coverage. Researchers should investigate the labour market consequences (for formal and informal sectors) associated with elimination/reduction and introduction/enhancement of labour market policies and regulations in different types of developing countries (e.g. minimum wages, dismissal notices and pension coverage). The assumption of many policy-makers, that such reductions are good and improvements are bad for labour market efficiency and national income growth (as well as being likely to increase informalization of the labour market), lacks empirical evidence; in addition, results will vary greatly depending on national conditions.

Many industrialized (OECD) countries are committed to increasing labour market "flexibility". Researchers should look systematically at all the available evidence which supports and/or refutes the labour flexibility argument; there is surprisingly little empirical evidence. Other important research topics include investigations of enterprise restructuring and its effect on vulnerable groups; and the relationship between globalization of production and the demand for unskilled workers, particularly those drawn from vulnerable groups.

In the transition economies, unfortunately, evidence is mounting that vulnerable groups are suffering disproportionately. It is thus important for researchers to monitor how vulnerable groups are faring in the transition period and to identify those most in need. Brief discussion followed of three "traditional" vulnerable groups and a number of research and policy suggestions made. There are considerable commonalities in terms of needs and policy requirements for these three quite different vulnerable groups:

1. All three groups are very heterogeneous as regards poverty and labour market disadvantages and it is necessary to subdivide each of these groups in order to devise appropriate poverty-oriented labour market policies and effective assistance. For example, we distinguished between child labourers and child workers; emphasized needs of women heading households and women working in female-dominated occupations (and industries) which have low pay/income; and distinguished between different types of disabled persons by their labour market disadvantages.

2. Heterogeneity implies the need for research to develop appropriate classification schemes, e.g. for disabled workers there is a need to develop a workable classification scheme based on labour market opportunities and disadvantages, which moves away from the present medical perspective.

3. Labour market policies for vulnerable groups should emphasize integrating members of the groups into the labour market and into non-traditional occupations with chances for promotion, responsibility and reasonable pay. (For children this could be interpreted as attending school.) Policies, programmes and projects which reinforce the segregation of workers in traditional jobs and occupations constitute a second-best approach to be avoided, except when required as a short-run solution to pressing poverty conditions.

4. In terms of research issues, it is important to collect and analyse detailed information on types of occupations and work activities of the disabled, children and women in order to observe where they are concentrated and their degree of occupational segregation. It would also be useful to investigate reasons for successful entry of disabled persons and women into what are now considered to be non-traditional occupations for them and to undertake impact evaluations and cost-effectiveness studies of projects and programmes. Such impact evaluations should ideally include a longitudinal aspect and perhaps tracer surveys.

5. To achieve integration skill development is critical, since to compete more effectively in the labour market the productivity of vulnerable groups needs improvement. This requires concentration on basic literacy for children and adults and vocational training and retraining for wage earners and persons interested in self-employment.

6. Integration requires non-labour market and labour market facilitating policies. These could include provision of community facilities, such as water taps, electricity and crèches; transport for disabled persons and local area development projects in areas with extensive child labour.

7. There is a need to undertake research which examines how and why vulnerable groups are disadvantaged in the labour market as seen from the employer's point of view, using establishment surveys, in-depth case studies and industry-level studies. For it is clear that labour market policies for vulnerable groups are more likely to succeed with the participation and cooperation of employers.

8. There is also a general need for improved labour market information and analysis and several suggestions in this regard have been made throughout the text of this chapter.

Labour market policies often focus on groups which are at a disadvantage and are discriminated against and these have already been defined, but designing general poverty-oriented labour market policies for such vulnerable groups is no easy matter. Not only do economic conditions, formalization of economies and governmental effectiveness differ from country to country, but cultural, historical and other country-specific factors also differ. However, despite these many variations, it is clear that there appear to be a significant number of similarities between countries in respect of a range of appropriate poverty-oriented labour market policies and action-oriented programmes for assisting vulnerable groups as well as a number of promising research topics.

Bibliographical references

Anker, R.; Hein, C. 1986. *Sex inequalities in urban employment in the Third World*. New York, Macmillan.

Anker, R.; et al. 1989. "Inequalities between men and women in nutrition and family welfare services: An in-depth enquiry in an Indian village", in Caldwell, J.; Santow, G.: *Selected readings in the cultural, social and behavioural determinants of health*. Canberra, Highland Press.

Anker, R.; Windell, J. Forthcoming. *Sex segregation of occupations around the world*.

Barbezat, D. 1993. *Occupational segregation by sex in the world. Equality for women in employment*. Working paper. Geneva, ILO.

Bardhan, P. 1989. "Poverty and employment characteristics of urban households in West Bengal, India: An analysis of the National Sample Survey, 1977-78", in Rodgers (ed.): *Urban poverty and the labour market*. Geneva, ILO.

Bilsborrow, R.; Degraff, D.; Anker, R. 1993. *Poverty monitoring and rapid assessment surveys*, mimeo.

Chamie, M. 1989. "Survey design strategies for the studying of disability", in *World Health Statistics Quarterly* (Geneva, World Health Organization), Vol. 42, No. 3.

Freeman, R. 1992. *Labour market institutions and policies: Help or hindrance to economic development*. Paper for the World Bank Annual Conference on Development Economics, Washington, DC, 30 April-1 May.

Goldschmidt-Clermont, L. 1990. "Economic measurement of non-market household activities: Is it useful and feasible", in *International Labour Review* (Geneva, ILO), Vol. 129, No. 3.

Gunderson, M. 1994. *Comparable worth and gender discrimination: International aspects*. Geneva, ILO.

Haddad, L.; Kanbar, R. 1990. "How serious is the neglect of intra-household inequality?", in *Economic Journal* (London, Cambridge University Press).

Hoeven, R. van der; Anker, R. (eds.). 1994. *Poverty Monitoring: An international concern*. New York, Macmillan.

ILO. 1983. *Convention concerning vocational rehabilitation and employment (disabled persons)*. Convention No. 159. Geneva, ILO.

—. 1992a. *Training and active labour market policies*. Paper prepared for the ILO Governing Body Committee on Employment and Social Policy, November. Geneva, ILO.

—. 1992b. *World Labour Report*. Geneva, ILO.

—. 1993. *Active labour market policies in a wider policy context.* Paper prepared for ILO Governing Body Committee on Employment and Social Policy, November. Geneva, ILO.

—. 1993a. *The framework of ILO action against poverty,* mimeo. Geneva, ILO.

—. 1993b. *Towards the abolition of child labour: ILO policy and its implications for technical co-operation activities,* mimeo. Geneva, ILO.

—. CEET-Budapest. 1993. *Policy manual: Disabled workers in Central and Eastern Europe,* mimeo. Budapest, September.

Khan, M. E.; Anker, R.; Ghosh-Dastidar, S. K.; Patel, B. C. 1992. "Methodological issues in collecting time use data for female labour force", in *The Indian Journal of Labour Economics* (Lucknow), Vol. 35, No. 1.

Nugent, J.; Anker, R. 1990. "Old age support and fertility", *World Employment Programme Research Working Paper* No. 172.

OECD, 1990. *Labour market policies for the 1990s.* Paris, OCDE.

—. 1992. *Employment policies for people with disabilities: Report by an evaluation panel,* Paris, OECD.

—. 1993. *Employment outlook,* Paris, OECD.

Oppong, C.; Abu, K. 1987. *Seven roles of women,* ILO Women, Work and Development Series No. 13. Geneva, ILO.

Paukert, L. 1993. *Women's employment in East and Central Europe during the transition period,* mimeo. Geneva, ILO.

Rodgers, G. (ed.). 1989. *Urban poverty and the labour market.* Geneva, ILO.

Rubery, J.; Fagan, C. 1993. *Wage determination and sex segregation in the European Community: Summary.* Report of network of experts for Equal Opportunities Unit of the Commission of the European Communities, Brussels.

Standing, G.; Sziraczki, G.; Windell, J. 1992. "Impact of employment restructuring on disadvantaged groups in Bulgaria and Hungary", in *International Labour Review* (Geneva, ILO), Vol. 131, Nos. 4-5.

Standing, G. 1989. "Global feminisation through flexible labour", in *Labour market analysis and employment planning, working paper No. 31.* Geneva, ILO.

United Nations. Various years. *Human development report.* New York, United Nations.

United Nations, UN Statistics Office. 1990. *Disability statistics compendium.* New York, United Nations.

Webster's Dictionary. 1987. New York, Lexicon Publications.

World Bank. 1993. *World Development Report.* Washington, DC, World Bank.

4   Social security options for developing countries

LDC's
ᴑIS
HSS

S. Guhan[1]

The debate on social security in developing countries has emerged largely since the 1980s, prompted by several factors. One was the acknowledgement of the glaring dichotomy in the availability of social security between the industrial and developing countries; and, not unrelated to this, the dichotomy between the access to social security in the developing countries themselves for labour in the organized sectors of public and industrial employment vis-à-vis the vast majority in the unorganized rural and urban sectors. The second was the realization that even the portfolio of direct poverty alleviation measures cannot be depended upon to provide adequate, timely or guaranteed protection to insure the poor against identifiable forms of deprivation. The third, and more proximate, factor has been the recognition of the role of social safety nets in cushioning the poor during the structural adjustment which many developing countries initiated in the 1980s in response to the debt crisis or as part of domestic economic reform processes. Parallel with these trends, the literature on poverty in the 1980s has paid much greater attention to its relationship with risk and vulnerability. The decade has also seen an extensive appraisal of country experiences in poverty alleviation. These trends appear to strike chords with one another at different pitches. Policy and need call for the location of specific social security entitlements within the anti-poverty framework, while theorizing relates anti-poverty measures to an over-arching notion of social security.

Drawing from conceptual insights and from empirical lessons provided by country experiences, it is necessary to formulate working definitions for social security in developing countries and to translate them into an agenda

[1] Emeritus Professor, Madras Institute of Development Studies. This is an abridged version of a paper with the same title presented at the symposium on "Poverty: New approaches to analysis and policy" organized by the International Institute for Labour Studies, Geneva, 22-24 November 1993.

for practical action. This is necessary for informing national policies, for providing the basis for normative recommendations from international agencies, and for guiding international cooperation in the relief of deprivation.

This chapter is an exploration of the possible contents of such an agenda. Organized in five sections, it first discusses the limitations of the formal security model to developing countries and then the elements of what could constitute appropriate social security for poor countries. Thirdly, the cost effectiveness of the principal approaches is reviewed. The fourth section is devoted to three generic issues: targeting, resources and administration. Finally, an agenda based on the earlier discussion is set out.

I. Formal social security and developing countries

The sense of the term "formal social security" used here is as codified in ILO Convention No. 102 (1952) covering the nine branches of social security; medical care and benefits addressed to sickness, unemployment, old age, employment injury, family size, maternity, invalidity and widow- hood.[2] The extent and coverage of formal social security in developing countries suffer from a number of shortcomings. In the first instance, their mere availability varies considerably across contingencies. Work injury benefits are available in most developing countries. Benefits for old age, disability and to survivors are also prevalent in fair measure. Availability of schemes covering sickness or maternity is more restricted; even more so are family allowance schemes. Few developing countries provide unemployment benefits. Secondly, most of the schemes cover only workers in the government and quasi-government sectors and workers in organized employment in mining, manufacturing or plantations where the workforce is stable, employment is regular and a clear employer-employee nexus exists. Large segments of workers in the agricultural sector, in rural non-farm employment, and in the urban informal sector are excluded. Thirdly, the regional dispersion of formal social security is very uneven in the Third World. It is relatively well-developed in the highly urbanized, middle-

---

[2] Related ILO Conventions are the Medical Care and Sickness Benefits Convention, 1969 (No. 130); the Invalidity, Old Age and Survivors' Benefits Convention, 1967 (No. 128); the Employment Injury Benefits Convention, 1964 (No. 121); the Maternity Protection (Revised) Convention, 1952 (No. 103); the Occupational Safety and Health Convention, 1981 (No. 155).

income countries of Latin America and the Caribbean (LAC) while outside the LAC region (with few exceptions) its availability is very restricted. Fourthly, formal social security systems are malfunctional in several ways. Evasion of employer liabilities is widespread (e.g. for work injury and maternity). The regular and timely collection of contributions from the insured and their employers is not easy. Provident funds do not provide adequate retirement benefits. Administrative overheads are high. Disbursement is delayed and is subject to cumbersome procedures. Many schemes have also run into actuarial and fiscal imbalances [ILO, 1993, pp. 57-61; Mesa-Lago, 1991].

1. Limitations of the formal model

Clearly an exclusive reliance on formal systems would be inappropriate in developing countries for several reasons stemming both from their levels of economic development and the structures of their economies. Fundamentally, the diagnosis of poverty in industrial countries from which formal systems are derived is not applicable to low-income developing countries since in their case the incidence of poverty is high, has been persistent over time and is rooted in several structural features of their economies.

Moreover, while the nature and magnitude of deprivation in the poor countries indicate a massive need for intervention of some sort, several limitations render the conventional formal model of social security inapplicable. Credit and insurance markets are underdeveloped, restricting the scope for private insurance. The scope for social insurance is limited because the labour market is characterized by high proportions of self-employment and unstable and irregular wage employment. While this implies a predominant role for social assistance provided through the budget, tax resources (especially from direct taxes on incomes) are limited. At the same time, competing demands on budgetary resources — for capital outlays on infrastructure and on primary education and primary health care, for example — insistently use up resources that would otherwise be available for social transfers. The resource constraint combined with the objective of covering all the needy entails targeting through income testing. However, given the irregularity of incomes and the diversity of their sources characterizing the populations concerned, the measurement of incomes is a daunting task in developing countries.

Two other features which render formal models inappropriate in this context are the intractability of the problems represented by the needy themselves and of unemployment as a cause of loss or interruption of income. Rural populations are spatially scattered, occupationally diffuse and difficult to reach administratively. High occupational diversity and employment instability occur in the urban informal sector as well. Much unemployment is underemployment (irregular employment of short duration, diverse jobs) rather than the frictional and cyclical "open" unemployment normally experienced in industrial economies. Nor are unemployment and poverty congruent: the poor in developing countries are poor not because they lack employment (in fact, they are overworked) but because they are employed irregularly at low wages or derive low incomes from self-employment based on low assets. All in all, in the words of two leading authorities on the subject, it does not make sense to regard the social programmes of France, the United Kingdom and the United States as presenting a shop window from which a developing country can select the goods it prefers. Neither Beveridge nor Bismarck nor Roosevelt can provide a model for social security in developing countries [Atkinson & Hills, 1991, p. 103].

II. Social security appropriate to developing countries

The negative conclusion that developing countries cannot rely on the formal model *alone* for social security provision implies in essence that social security in poor countries will have to be viewed as part of and fully integrated with anti-poverty policies, with such policies themselves being broadly conceived in view of the complex, multi-dimensional nature of poverty and deprivation. The conceptual problem is to situate an operationally useful notion of social security — one that is neither excessively specific (as in the formal model) nor excessively general — *within* a comprehensive anti-poverty approach.[3] From this standpoint, a categorization of the instruments I consider relevant for poverty alleviation may be useful. There are three broad categories: *promotional* measures that aim to improve endowments, exchange entitlements, real incomes and social consumption; *preventive* measures that seek more directly to avert deprivation in specific ways; and *protective* (or safety-net) measures that are yet more specific in their objective of guaranteeing relief from deprivation.

This is a taxonomy with overlapping categories. Works programmes, for instance, promote employment; they can also be seen as preventing

---

[3] For comprehensive approaches to social security see Sen [1981; 1983; 1985]; Dreze & Sen [1989; 1991]; and Burgess & Stern [1991].

unemployment. Health care promotes well-being; it may also prevent sickness. The value of these categories does not, therefore, lie in their being clear-cut or mutually exclusive. My purpose is rather to suggest a gradation of measures that proceed, like a set of concentric circles, from wider to narrower domains of specificity, while recognizing that all three types of measures are called for. The outer circle of promotional measures would include the whole array of macro-economic, sectoral and institutional measures of major importance for poverty reduction, operating at the macro and meso levels. Though oriented towards the poor, they may not be confined to them or addressed specifically to the prevention of actual types of deprivation (for example, primary education, primary health care, child nutrition, slum improvement). The middle circle would consist of what have come to be known as direct measures for poverty alleviation, such as asset redistribution, employment creation, and food security. The inner circle would contain specific measures for the relief from or protection against deprivation to the extent that the latter is not — or cannot be — averted through promotional and preventive approaches.

This visualization helps clarify several questions. The first is that social security provision in developing countries requires a multiple approach. The second arises from the residual nature of safety nets; poverty must be alleviated as much as possible by the outer circles of promotional and preventive measures so that the burden on safety nets can be lessened. Thirdly, safety nets must indeed act as the last resort as regards any entitlements.

III. Relevant preventive and protective measures

1. Scope and limitations of the discussion

Using this frame, one can appropriately limit the following discussion to the set of preventive and protective measures most relevant for social security provision in developing countries. Broadly, these include *(a)* measures to provide assets; *(b)* measures to improve exchange entitlements; and *(c)* specifically protective, safety-net measures.

As well as identifying the programmes involved, it is necessary to assess their effectiveness in terms of quantifiable indicators. The limitations of data being what they are, any such attempt will be crude but it can be useful in broadly differentiating between the sheep and the goats. In this spirit, I have used five broad indicators wherever, and to the extent, possible. The first is the *coverage ratio*, which is simply the coverage in a specific programme of the contingency or need to which it is purportedly addressed (e.g. poverty alleviation, employment, old-age relief, etc.). The coverage depends both on the budgetary outlay and the take-up by intended beneficiaries. Secondly, the *transfer efficiency*, which is the proportion of the likely net benefit to one unit of gross expenditure, after allowing for programme and administrative overheads, administrative leakages and any other offsets. Thirdly, the *targeting efficiency*, which is the proportion of the transfer that reaches its target group after allowing for the share going to those outside the target group either explicitly (as in universal schemes) or because of leakages. This is equivalent to the concept of vertical targeting efficiency.[4] Fourth is the *benefit-cost ratio*, which is the product of transfer efficiency and targeting efficiency. It seeks to indicate how much the target group is likely to benefit in the final outcome from one unit of expenditure. Fifth is the *impact efficiency*, which is the product of the coverage ratio and the benefit-cost ratio. As the broadest indicator, it gives an idea of the overall impact of any specific programme after taking into account outlay and take-up, vertical and horizontal efficiencies, and overheads and leakages.

Two caveats are necessary in respect of the scope of this chapter. The more important schemes are discussed at some length in preference to comprehensive coverage. Several important aspects of social security have been omitted: famine prevention and famine relief — because the subject has been definitively dealt with by Dreze and Sen [Dreze & Sen, 1989, Part II]. Another type of extraordinary deprivation is that caused by wars, a subject on which not much light has been cast.[5] The meeting of basic needs, especially in health care and education, is vital to social security; the literature on this is extensive and easily accessible [ILO, 1976; Streeten et al., 1981; Stewart, 1985; Ron et al., 1990; UNDP, 1993 and earlier; World Bank, 1993]. Besides, as far as the poor are concerned, the measures involved are largely promotional, while the focus of this paper is on protection. Social security under conditions of structural adjustment has been the subject of much recent discussion; here again, there is adequate and accessible literature [Cornia et al., 1987; Burgess et al., 1993]. Furthermore, structural adjustment only accentuates the need for social security and does not basically alter the types of protection required. Finally, there is traditional, informal and familial social security, on which

---

[4] Vertical efficiency involves covering *only* those in the target group and horizontal efficiency involves covering *all* those in the target group. See Weisbrod [1969].

[5] Stewart [1993] contains an excellent discussion of magnitudes and issues.

again the literature is good though mostly anthropological (see Platteau [1991] for a survey).

The second caveat relates to the fact that for reasons of space much of the empirical material relied upon comes from India. India has a very large weight among developing countries in both population (about 20 per cent) and in rural poverty (about 30 per cent). Secondly, Indian programmes for social security provision have operated on a fairly large scale and over a fairly long period, have encompassed a variety of interventions, and have attracted a considerable evaluative literature. As such, they can potentially provide models for other low-income countries.

With this clarification of the scope and with these caveats in mind, we turn to the examination of the most salient programmes for social security provision in developing countries.

2. Access to land

In the agricultural economy, land is the primary asset from a subsistence point of view. It provides food security, enables utilization of family labour, and reduces vulnerability to labour and food markets. Land redistribution is important not only for providing the rural poor with a primary asset but also from the point of view of deconcentrating the economic and political power of large landlords which enables them to reduce wages, increase rents, operate in interlocked credit markets, and exercise diverse forms of extra-economic oppression over the poor [Bell, 1990]. In India and Bangladesh land reform has been prominent on the agenda but actual implementation has fallen far short of original promises and objectives, reflecting the difficulty of reformist redistribution by autonomous and stable governments [Osmani, 1991].

The example of China shows how access to land can provide the fundamental basis for social security in an agrarian economy. As Ahmad and Hussain point out:

Land reform has been the most fundamental of the transformations... The shift back to family farming since 1979 has reversed collective farming but not the essential feature of the land reform: guaranteeing all rural households access to land... [Land reform] eliminated landlessness as a cause of destitution. Herein lies a crucial difference between the attributes of the rural poor in China and those in most other developing countries, where rural poverty and landlessness often go together [Ahmad & Hussain, 1991, pp. 263-264].

This example illustrates why land reform must continue to have a high priority in the social security agenda; it cannot be dismissed as a lost cause. To maintain political pressure for land reform and circumvent opposition, the credit mechanism is one means of facilitating land transfers from rich to poor. As land-owning households tend to convert landed assets into urban property and financial assets, tenants, small farmers and rural craftsmen tend to accumulate savings which could be supplemented with credit for land purchase, and natural market processes could be made redistributive.[6] Availability of credit can also prevent divestiture of land and other assets (livestock, implements), thus playing an important safety-net function. Concurrently, preservation and expansion of common property resources (land, forests, grazing areas, fisheries) are important aspects of social security which thus should not be neglected [Jodha, 1986; Agarwal, 1991].

3. Asset creation

The example of India's Integrated Rural Development Programme (IRDP) shows a large-scale, country-wide intervention designed to create assets for the poor so as to generate incomes via self-employment. In operation since 1978, this scheme finances a variety of investments through a combination of loans and subsidies for households whose incomes fall under a stipulated poverty line: Irrigation wells, milch cattle, draught animals, other livestock, poultry, carts and facilities for small-scale production, trade and services. Currently, 3 to 4 million rural households are targeted annually for benefits under the IRDP, with cumulative cover-age being some 30 million households.

More than a decade of experience and numerous evaluations have drawn attention to a variety of shortcomings in the IRDP,[7] which can be summarized as follows:

(1) Targeting to poor households is weak, with the result that a substantial proportion of actual beneficiaries are the ineligible non-poor.

(2) Beneficiaries below the poverty line tend to cluster just below it, with only a small proportion of them being the poorest of the poor.

(3) Incomes that the assets might generate are mostly used for current consumption, especially in emergencies such as droughts, sickness or death, with the result that beneficiaries either fall into a debt trap or are forced to default on repayments.

---

[6] For an interesting proposal in this connection see Bell [1990, p. 158]. See also, Guhan [1988, p. 201].

[7] For a collection of evaluations, see Krishnaswamy [1990, Part III].

(4) External, complementary support services are inadequate for dependable streams of income to be derived from the assets provided to the poor. Nilakantha Rath estimates that, altogether, after the first seven years of the operation (1978-85), only "about 3 per cent of the poor households in rural India would have been helped to live above poverty, even if for a while only" [Rath, 1985]. The impact ratio in the IRDP is thus very low.

Each of these findings illustrates important issues in social security provision: (1) and (2) show that means-tested targeting through administrative mechanisms is not likely to be efficient, either vertically or horizontally; (3) indicates that anti-poverty programmes need protective safety nets if they are to succeed; and (4) draws attention to the importance of externalities and the futility, in their absence, of micro household approaches to poverty alleviation.

4. Employment

Direct employment generation for the rural poor is sometimes viewed as a prime instrument of poverty alleviation and social security provision. Large schemes for providing employment for rural unskilled labour have been in operation in India and in Bangladesh for nearly two decades. India has had a nation-wide scheme since 1977 but an earlier, more intensive and widely reported example is the Employment Guarantee Scheme (EGS) in the State of Maharashtra which has been in operation since 1972. The Food for Work Programme (FFWP) in Bangladesh was started soon after the 1974 famine and has expanded since then. In the late 1980s, each of these schemes provided about 100 million person-days of employment annually. Both use labour for the creation of a variety of communal assets: irrigation works, roads, soil conservation, afforestation, small buildings. Wages are paid in cash in the EGS and mostly in kind (imported wheat from food aid) in the FFWP.[8]

Rural employment schemes have a great deal in their favour. They link the creation of rural assets to providing supplementary employment for unskilled labour. In social security terms, their most important contribution is the stabilization and ensuring of incomes in lean seasons, droughts and famines, providing immediate relief as well as protection against costlier adjustments such as the sale of land and assets. By way of poverty

---

[8] For an account of the South Asian schemes see Osmani [1991, pp. 330-338]. On employment schemes in other countries see ILO [1992].

alleviation, they improve exchange entitlements for small farmers and the landless who constitute 70 to 80 per cent of the rural poor in most developing countries and whose only endowment is labour power.

Employment schemes have been advocated not only as a useful form of social security intervention but also on the grounds that they have an outstanding characteristic making them preferable to other modalities.[9] This lies in the property of self-selection, the importance of which as a desideratum in poverty alleviation is based on the savings in administrative costs and the difficulty in obtaining accurate information. Given these information and agency problems, there is no satisfactory alternative to shifting the costs of selection on to the participants themselves by imposing on them the costs of any income foregone through their participation, of travel to and residence at work sites, and of extra nutrition. Inasmuch as such costs are likely to be lower for the poor, a works programme is self-selecting.[10]

The a priori appeal of employment schemes is, however, seriously undermined by empirical evidence relating to the Maharashtra EGS, a prime example of this form of intervention. The overall impact of the EGS has been estimated to affect only 2.5 per cent of unemployment among all rural workers [Mahendra Dev, 1992, pp. 46-47]. This is despite budgetary outlays for the scheme amounting to as much as 10 per cent of Maharashtra's total developmental expenditure. In other words, the EGS is far from providing an employment guarantee, despite entailing a relatively high budgetary outlay.

Benefits to the poor from one person-day of employment will be a function of the targeting efficiency under the scheme and the wage income actually transferred less the foregone income. Available studies suggest that the EGS performs well in terms of its targeting efficiency; 80 to 90 per cent of participants are likely to be under the poverty line. The nominal wage component in the total cost involved in creating a person-day of employment was about 50 per cent in the late 1980s, but there is evidence that wages actually received by workers were less on account of corruption and manipulation in the piece-rate wage system. Allowing for this factor, the ratio of the actual transfer via wages to the total cost may turn out to be 30 to 40 per cent. Ravallion estimates foregone incomes alone in the range of 40 to 50 per cent of wages received [Ravallion, 1990a, p. 27].

---

[9] For a vigorous advocacy of employment programmes, especially in the famine prevention context, see Dreze & Sen [1989, pp. 113-118].

[10] For an exposition of these arguments see Ravallion [1990, pp. 7-13].

Assuming the best estimates for all three parameters (90 per cent coverage of the poor, 40 per cent for the wage component and 40 per cent for foregone incomes) the benefit-cost ratio turns out to be 21.6 per cent (0.9 x 0.4 x 0.6), i.e. overheads (administrative and material costs), leakages, foregone incomes and the targeting factor consume about 80 per cent of the gross outlay. Thus, despite self-selection having a high targeting efficiency, any other mode of transfer in which the information, agency and other deadweight losses are likely to be less than about 80 per cent can, in principle, be more cost-effective.

The poor can derive indirect benefits from the assets created under the EGS but only on two conditions: the assets must be durable (not just roads that are washed away in the next rains) and they should be such as to benefit the poor (at least along with the non-poor). Available studies indicate that non-durable rather than more permanent works tend to be preferred for a variety of reasons: the dispersion of the works, the tendency to economize on materials in order to increase the wage content, and local political pressures. In many cases, works are abandoned incomplete and new ones started elsewhere; and maintenance is sorely neglected [Mahendra Dev, 1992, pp. 52-53]. Furthermore, assets such as irrigation, soil conservation and roads are likely, by their very nature, to benefit the land-owning and trading non-poor rather than those who have laboured to create them. Second-run benefits can also occur if the EGS wages have the effect of raising normal agricultural wages by providing a counter for other agricultural workers. For this to happen, EGS works need to be undertaken during normal agricultural operations but if they are, the dilemma is that they will not be able to ensure incomes in the lean season of peak unemployment. A further dilemma is that if, in order to provide the bargaining strength, EGS wages are kept above normal agri-cultural wages, this will conflict with the objective of maximizing employment from a given budgetary outlay.

Some broad conclusions can be drawn from employment schemes. One is that they may have a small impact on rural unemployment and poverty despite large budgetary outlays; they leave out, in any case, the unemployable such as the old and the handicapped and do not have an urban equivalent. Secondly, it becomes necessary to keep wages low so as to be able to capture the neediest and to maximize employment; this could, however, erode the extent of relief. Thirdly, the assets to be created need to be durable and of a kind that can be expected to benefit the poor through growth, rural-urban linkages or more directly. This involves local-level prioritization, planning and the sequencing of public works.[11] Fourthly, the need for administrative efficiency and to reduce corruption and leakages is as strong in works programmes as it is in other forms of transfer which entail administrative selection. Fifthly, while self-selection may result in a high targeting efficiency in employment schemes, their benefit-cost ratio is not so attractive as to exclude serious consideration of direct transfers.

5. *Minimum wages*

If enforced, minimum wages can offer vastly greater potential for transfers than employment schemes such as the EGS, which pay an equivalent of less than a minimum wage.

Received wisdom would discourage faith in minimum wages, with excess labour supply, labour substitution through mechanization and/or changes in the cropping pattern, enforcement problems, opposition from rural oligarchies and so on. Yet, there is no reason why the room for manœuvre in wage up-gradation should not be probed through such measures as: (i) making widely available information on minimum wages and on penalties for non-compliance; (ii) specific emphasis on enforcing minimum wages for time-bound activities, such as harvesting, sowing, transplanting, etc., in which both the bargaining strength of labour is relatively strong and wages earned amount to a sizeable proportion of annual wage incomes; (iii) adequate and motivated enforcement machinery; (iv) the establishment of local wage-monitoring committees with representation from male and female agricultural labourers; (v) encouragement to NGOs working in this field; (vi) in-season public works in low-wage pockets (see also Shaheed [1993]).

6. *Food subsidies*

Many developing countries have intervened in the food market through public distribution systems (PDS) and food subsidies linked to them and there is an extensive literature on country experiences in food security, PDS and food subsidies.[12] Our discussion will be limited to reviewing experience with the PDS and related food subsidies in India.

---

[11] This aspect is stressed in a number of contributions in ILO [1992] and by Osmani [1991]. In the Indian context, see Dantwala [1985].

[12] For an overview see World Bank [1986]. For China, Ahmad & Hussain [1991]; India and Bangladesh, Osmani [1991]; Sri Lanka, Edirisinghe [1987].

The Indian PDS handles 10 to 15 per cent of food grain availability in the country and is almost wholly based on domestically procured stocks. There are wide variations in its functioning in different states in India. In addition to the food subsidy provided by central Government, some of the states also subsidize grain. In general, entitlement to a ration card is universal, i.e. not targeted on the poor. Leakages occur at different points in the distribution chain and are estimated at up to 35 per cent of the gross amount of grain distributed [World Bank, 1992, p. 83]. At the central level alone, overheads currently amount to 57 per cent of the value of subsidy. Based on these estimates, Table 1 compares the benefit-cost ratio in the PDS with that in the Maharashtra EGS and indicates that this ratio in the PDS is probably only half of that in the employment programme, although the transfer efficiency in the PDS is somewhat higher. This is because targeting efficiency in the PDS is less than half as good as in self-targeting employment. However, the PDS has a much wider coverage than the EGS: even if its effective coverage is taken as being confined to the urban population in India (27 per cent), its impact ratio (11.2 per cent of 27 per cent, or 3 per cent) will be twice that in the EGS (21.6 per cent of 7 per cent, or 1.5 per cent).

School meal and child nutrition schemes can be viewed both as food security and as forms of family allowance which ease the burden of child rearing. They can also improve school enrolment and attendance.

Table 1: Comparison of cost-effectiveness in the Employment Guarantee Schemes (EGS) and Public Distribution Systems (PDS) in India

	EGS	PDS
1. Budgetary cost	100 [1]	100 [2]
2. Overheads	50 [3]	37 [4]
3. Leakage	10 [5]	35 [6]
4. Gross benefit (1 − 2 − 3)	40	28
5. Participation cost	16 [7]	Neg [8]
6. Net benefit (4 − 5) i.e. transfer efficiency	24	28
7. Targeting efficiency (coverage of poor)	0.9	0.4
8. Final transfer to poor (6 x 7) (benefit-cost ratio)	21.6	11.2

Notes: [1] Aggregate cost for creating one person-day of employment. [2] Cost of food subsidy. [3] Administrative overheads and non-labour expenditures. [4] Distribution overheads such as freight, storage costs, interest, etc. being 57 per cent of 65 per cent reaching consumers. [5] Underpayment of wages. [6] In transit and at points of sale. [7] Foregone earnings. [8] Ignoring foregone earnings due to waiting time and transport costs to retail shops.

7.   Social assistance

The main elements of social assistance are: targeting of the poor; need-based minimal assistance; tax financing; and protection as a matter of entitlement.[13] In the light of the relative neglect of social assistance, it may be useful to begin with a few general considerations that underline its importance and necessity. First, it is clear that contingent poverty arising from circumstances such as large family size, unemployment, old age, sickness, disability, maternity, and widowhood is often a part of chronic poverty; such circumstances both accentuate chronic poverty and can be accentuated by it. Secondly, it is not true that promotional measures, if implemented on a sufficiently large scale and over a sufficiently long time, will reduce the need for protection in the case of *all* contingencies. While, for instance, unemployment and sickness can be ameliorated through the provision of employment and health care, old age, (reasonable) maternity, and death cannot be prevented through measures promoting, for example, eternal youth, immaculate conception and immortality! Poverty in such contingencies, if it is to be tackled at all, has to be tackled through direct relief. Thirdly, while budgetary constraints are important, they have to be looked at in the overall framework of fiscal management: raising resources, curtailing unessential expenditures, greater equity in the mobilization and use of resources, and so on. Fourthly, promotion measures share almost all of the problems associated with protective measures since these problems are inherent to all direct anti-poverty programmes: low coverage, lax targeting, high overheads, leakage, low benefit-cost ratios. Furthermore, information and agency problems occur in any form of social provision. There is no reason to assume that such problems in social assistance schemes will be so serious as to disqualify direct transfers altogether. On the other hand, social assistance could have a reasonably high targeting efficiency precisely because it is contingency-related.

8.   Candidates for social assistance

Against this background, it is useful to recall the nine main branches of social security covered in ILO Convention No. 102 and to consider how efforts can be made to provide them to the poor not covered by formal security. Clearly unemployment, family support and sickness have to be tackled largely through promotional measures, viz., employment schemes,

---

[13] ILO [1942] defines social assistance as "a service or scheme which provides benefits to persons of small means as of right in amounts sufficient to meet minimum standards of need and financed from taxation".

child nutrition and health care. The five other contingencies (old age, widowhood, maternity, disability and employment injury) need to be tackled, if at all, through social assistance.

There is sufficient empirical evidence to argue confidently that these five contingencies can be feasibly covered by social assistance in terms of meeting minimum standards of need, even in India. Means-tested old-age pensions for the poor were first introduced in India at the state level in 1957. In subsequent decades, almost all the states in India have introduced old-age pension schemes for the poor above the age of 60 or 65. In addition to general old-age pension schemes, many states have more liberal schemes for agricultural labourers who are likely to be the poorest in the elderly population. Pensions are also available in most states for widows and for the physically handicapped in the form of survivor and disability benefits. Some states provide survivor, disability and employment injury benefits to families or victims involved in specified hazardous occupations such as fishing, construction work, tree-tapping, well-digging, pesticide-spraying, tractor-driving, loading and so on.

There is wide variation in the coverage, benefits and eligibility conditions among the states and also in implementation efficiency and take-up.[14] However, two states in India — Kerala and Tamil Nadu — have demonstrated the viability and potential of such schemes. The Kerala pension scheme has been estimated to cover almost all of the target group of the elderly poor and some form of social assistance is available to half the workers in the unorganized sector [United Nations, 1992]. The current social assistance package in Tamil Nadu includes pensions for old age, agricultural labourers, widows and the physically handicapped, survivor benefits, maternity assistance and accident relief. All households below the poverty level are eligible under these schemes except in the case of pensions where means-testing is more stringent. In both states, pensions are likely to meet 50 per cent or more of subsistence requirements; the survivor benefit in Tamil Nadu may amount to about six months' earnings or more for a poor household; and maternity assistance may equal three months' wages for a female agricultural labourer. It has been estimated that about 17 per cent of poor households in Tamil Nadu are protected from contingencies which, without these schemes, might have immiserized them in extreme poverty, if not in absolute destitution. A very high proportion of beneficiaries are women (nearly 60 per cent) [Guhan, 1992a].

---

[14] On Indian social assistance schemes, see Guhan [1992c, p. 287].

A detailed evaluation suggests that, despite stringent means-testing, about a third of the elderly poor proved eligible for old-age pensions in Tamil Nadu in 1990. The coverage was 60 to 70 per cent in the case of maternity assistance and survivor benefits.[15] The targeting efficiency was high for three reasons. The benefits are small enough for the non-poor to desist from infiltrating into the eligible group, risking stigma at the local level. Secondly, no ceilings were placed on the number of eligible beneficiaries; accordingly, infiltration by the non-poor does not displace the poor from benefits. Thirdly, income status is more reliably verified on the basis of local enquiries while deciding on claims and not on a prior wholesale basis for large populations, as in the case of the Indian IRDP. The transfer efficiency is also high. Moral hazard — the incentive to make less effort to avoid the contingency covered — does not pose a serious problem here: it is impossible in the case of old age; maternity assistance is limited to the first two births; and the survivor benefit provides no special incentive for spouse murder. Overheads are low (3 to 5 per cent) because claims are verified by the regular government staff. Disbursements are made through the post office in order to prevent corruption at this stage. Thus, on all accounts, contingency-related social assistance in this model fares much better in terms of its cost-benefit ratio than even "self-targeted" employment schemes.

Extrapolating the Tamil Nadu package to the all-India level, I have demonstrated elsewhere that a nation-wide "minimum relevant" social assistance package of old-age pensions, survivor benefits, accident relief and maternity assistance for poor households is likely to cost no more than 0.3 per cent of India's GDP and about 1 per cent of the combined revenues of the central and state Governments in India [Guhan, 1992b]. Even with an increasing proportion of the elderly in the process of demographic change, the cost-to-GDP ratio in real terms will remain at about the same level in future decades. The minimum package can thus be both affordable and sustainable.

---

[15] Guhan [1992a]. It is interesting that the proportions of the aged poor covered by pensions in Kerala and Tamil Nadu are much higher than the 3 per cent reported for China in Ahmad and Hussain [1991, p. 274]. The very low coverage in China can perhaps be explained by stringent means-testing and the stigma associated with *wubao* relief to some extent but the major explanation could be that access to land and grain relief in China have greatly reduced the demand on *wubao* relief. Ahmad and Hussain are not, however, right in asserting that "in most developing economies, public provisions for the indigent elderly in rural areas simply do not exist and that the coverage in China is exceptional for a developing economy".

IV. Three generic issues

1. Targeting

The issue of targeting is central to budget-financed social assistance transfers. The search is for mechanisms that can achieve the widest coverage of the target group (maximizing horizontal efficiency) by concentrating benefits on them (maximizing vertical efficiency). Although the two types of efficiency will generally move in the same direction, this may not always happen since, within a given budgetary ceiling, there are two kinds of trade-off. One is between the administrative costs involved in targeting and the outlay available for benefits (programme costs). The other is between such administrative costs and vertical targeting efficiency. Although reducing administrative costs may lower vertical efficiency, it will increase programme outlays for a given budgetary allocation; and larger programme outlays can conceivably improve horizontal efficiency. Thus, a trade-off between vertical and horizontal targeting efficiencies can emerge. Furthermore, political economy considerations call for a wide spread of benefits, which requires (near-)universal schemes with low overheads, large programme outlays and a sacrifice of vertical efficiency. Horizontal efficiency in such schemes may be less than in more closely targeted schemes but not proportionately so, because of the larger programme outlays available. In other words, the price to be paid in efficiency for political sustainability may not be excessive.[16]

The ideal in targeting is to achieve both efficiency and equity by both minimizing administrative overheads *and* maximizing vertical efficiency. The quest for this optimum implies two broad approaches. One is to bypass administrative selection through resort to self-targeting schemes (e.g. employment schemes). The other is to tackle directly the information and agency problems involved in administrative selection so as to reduce their costs and/or improve their efficiency. The proposals made from this point of view include resort to indicator targeting using a variety of surrogates for income-testing: landlessness or marginal land ownership; residence in disadvantaged locations; consumption of foods generally eaten by the poor; age (pensions for the old and nutrition for the very young); sex (support for maternity, post-natal assistance and widowhood), and so on. Means-testing itself can be improved by excluding the obviously non-poor on the

---

[16] There is an extensive literature on targeting. For discussion and further references see Kanbur & Besley [1990]; Kumar & Stewart [1992, pp. 269-274]; and Lipton & Ravallion [1993, pp. 58-60].

basis of easily identifiable characteristics such as ownership of land and property, liability to taxes, salaries and so on) rather than aiming at a precise identification of the poor. In the case of contingency-related social assistance, incomes can be more reliably verified since relief is sanctioned on a case-by-case basis after the event. Furthermore, a reduction in agency problems can be sought through administrative and participatory decentralization.

Finally, it must be remembered that the different types of social assistance scheme are not fungible. It is not meaningful to choose the most cost-effective among them for application across the board: each type of need calls for a specific form of relief. It is the optimal mix of schemes in terms of feasibility and appropriateness in meeting the spectrum of needs that will determine cost-effectiveness in the social security system as a whole. What is important, therefore, is not so much fine-tuned comparisons between alternatives but rather every attempt to reduce administrative overheads, leakage, corruption and other factors which undermine the targeting *and* transfer efficiencies in *all* major schemes. Good governance, alas, is inescapable.

2. *Financing*

There is no better maxim than "where there's a will, there's a way" to guide discussion of financing the fight against deprivation. Apart from the reduction of expenditure on other outlays (notably military expenditures and subsidies for the non-poor) and the reallocation of resources saved thereby for social security, it is also possible to raise additional resources for social security. Typically, social security payments (about 10 per cent of GDP) explain the major part of the difference between tax-to-GDP ratios in the developed countries (about 30 per cent of GDP) and in the developing ones (15 to 20 per cent). This indicates that if resources are not available for social security, it may be largely because the opportunity for mobilizing *and* spending *additional* resources that social security offers is being missed. Of course, every effort must be made towards containing costs and improving benefits in social assistance transfers, as this article has argued.

The Indian experience could suggest a broad indicative target for expenditures on social assistance. India's current outlay on the set of schemes referred to above adds up to about 1.5 per cent of its (1993)

GDP.[17] Prima facie, a doubling of this level of outlay, i.e. 3 per cent of GDP, would appear to be necessary as well as feasible.

3. Administration

The importance of decentralized delivery systems operating through local institutions in which the poor are not only enfranchised but empowered emerges from everything that has been discussed so far: reducing information and agency costs in targeting, micro-level planning for employment programmes, localized provision of credit, checking fraud and corruption at the root, quick settlement of claims, mobilizing local revenues. Most importantly, locally provided social security can be of fundamental importance in generating and sustaining "solidarity" which is the essence of social security.[18]

V. A proposed agenda

The agenda for "appropriate social security for developing countries" that emerges from this review can be summarized quite simply.

While formal social security systems cannot be exclusively relied upon in developing countries, it is necessary to reform them and to extend their application where and when appropriate.

Land redistribution must be placed and maintained at the forefront of the social security agenda. Even under reformist regimes, it may be possible to stimulate and facilitate land transfers from the rich to the poor, through the credit mechanism.

Credit can be of fundamental importance for preventing asset depletion, enabling the acquisition by the poor of land and other assets, and for providing working capital to the self-employed poor in rural and urban areas.

---

[17] My rough estimate.

[18] As Keith Griffin & Terry McKinley [1993, p. 72] eloquently point out: "Empowerment... is not only democratic, it may also be efficient. It calls for a streamlined central administration which devolves authority as much as possible to the local level. By enlisting the active participation of the people instead of relying on a cumbersome bureaucracy to 'deliver' services to beneficiaries who have little voice in what is delivered and how it is delivered, empowerment may actually be more cost-effective than the alternatives... Where this does occur, empowerment, human development and economic efficiency are inextricably intertwined. They are the principal components of a strategy that puts people first." See also UNDP [1993, Chs. 2, 4 and 5].

Rural employment schemes, wage upgrading for rural labour, food subsidies linked to public distribution systems, child nutrition and contingency-related support for old age, maternity, survivors and the disabled could constitute a minimal social assistance package. An optimal mix of these programmes focusing on both needs and cost-effectiveness would be necessary, though decision-makers must recognize that cost-effectiveness is a function not only of targeting efficiency but also of the transfer efficiency in specific schemes.

Prima facie, a target of 3 per cent of GDP for such basic minimum social security appears to be reasonable and affordable in most developing countries. Decentralized, participatory institutional arrangements would be essential.

Bibliographical references

Agarwal, B. 1991. "Social security and the family: Coping with seasonality and calamity in rural India", in Ahmad et al. (1991).

Ahmad, E.; Hussain, A. 1991. "Social security in China: A historical perspective", in Ahmad et al. (1991).

Atkinson, A. B.; Hills, G. 1991. "Social security in developed countries: Are there lessons for developing countries?", in Ahmad et al. (1991).

Bell, C. 1990. "Reforming property rights in land and tenancy", in *The World Bank Research Observer* (Washington, DC), Vol. 5, No. 2, July, pp. 143-166.

Burgess, R.; Stern, N. 1991. "Social security in developing countries: What, why, who and how?", in Ahmad et al. (1991).

Burgess, R.; Drèze, J.; Ferreira, F.; Hussain, A.; Thomas, J. 1993. *Social protection and structural adjustment*, mimeo. London, London School of Economics.

Cornia, G. A.; Jolly, R.; Stewart, F. (eds.). 1987. *Adjustment with a human face*. Oxford, Clarendon Press.

Dantwala, M. L. 1985. "Garibi Hatao: Strategy options", in *Economic and Political Weekly* (Bombay), Vol. XX, No. 11, pp. 475-476.

Drèze, J.; Sen, A. 1989. *Hunger and public action*. Oxford, Clarendon Press.

—. 1991. "Public action for social security: Foundations and strategy", in Ahmad et al. (1991).

Edirisinghe, N. 1987. *The food stamp scheme in Sri Lanka: Costs, benefits and options for modification*. Washington, DC, International Food Policy Research Institute.

Griffin, K.; McKinley, T. 1993. *Towards a human development strategy*. New York, UNDP.

Guhan, S. 1988. "Aid for the poor: Performance and possibilities in India", in Lewis, J. P. et al. (eds.): *Strengthening the poor: What have we learned?*. New Brunswick, Transaction Books.

—. 1992a. "Social security initiatives in Tamil Nadu, 1989", in Subramanian, S. (ed.): *Themes in development economics: Essays in honour of Malcolm S. Adiseshiah*. Delhi, Oxford University Press.

—. 1992b. *Social security for the unorganized poor: A feasible blueprint for India*, mimeo. Madras, Madras Institute of Development Studies.

—. 1992c. "Social security in India: Looking one step ahead", in Harriss et al. (1992).

Harriss, B.; Guhan, S.; Cassen, R. H. (eds.). 1992. *Poverty in India, research and policy*. Bombay, Oxford University Press.

ILO. 1942. *Approaches to social security: An international survey*. Montreal.

—. 1976. *Employment, growth and basic needs: A one-world problem*. Geneva.

—. 1992. *International Labour Review* (Geneva, ILO), Vol. 132, No. 1. Special issue on "Productive employment for the poor".

—. 1993. *World Labour Report* (Geneva, ILO).

Jodha, N. S. 1986. "Common property resources and rural poor", in *Economic and Political Weekly* (Bombay), Vol. XXI, 5 July.

Kanbur, R.; Besley, T. 1990. *The principles of targeting*. WPS No. 85. Washington, DC, World Bank.

Krishnaswamy, K. S. (ed.). 1990. *Poverty and income distribution*. Bombay, Oxford University Press.

Kumar, G.; Stewart, F. 1992. "Tackling malnutrition: What can targeted nutritional interventions achieve?", in Harriss et al. (1992).

Lipton, M.; Ravallion, M. 1993. *Poverty and policy*. WPS No. 1130. Washington, DC, World Bank.

Mahendra Dev, S. 1992. *Poverty alleviation programmes: A case study of Maharashtra with emphasis on Employment Guarantee Scheme*. Discussion Paper No. 7. Bombay, Indira Gandhi Institute of Development Research.

Mesa-Lago, C. 1991. "Social security in Latin America and the Caribbean: A comparative assessment", in Ahmad et al. (1991).

Osmani, S. R. 1991. "Social security in South Asia", in Ahmad et al. (1991).

Parikh, K. S. 1993. *Who gets how much from PDS: How effectively does it reach the poor?*. Bombay, Indira Gandhi Institute of Development Research.

Platteau, J.-P. 1991. "Traditional systems of social security and hunger insurance: Past achievements and modern challenges", in Ahmad et al. (1991).

Rath, N. 1985. "'Garibi Hatao': Can IDRP do it?", in *Economic and Political Weekly* (Bombay), Vol. XX, No. 6, pp. 238-246.

Ravallion, M. 1990. *Reaching the poor through rural public employment: A survey of theory and evidence*. World Bank Discussion Paper No. 94. Washington, DC, World Bank.

Ron, A.; Abel-Smith, B.; Tamburi, G. 1990. *Health insurance in developing countries: The social security approach*. Geneva, ILO.

Sen, A. 1981. *Poverty and famines: An essay on entitlement and deprivation*. Oxford, Clarendon Press.

—. 1983. "Development: Which way now?", in *The Economic Journal* (Cambridge), Vol. 93, Dec. pp. 745-762.

—. 1985. *Commodities and capabilities*. Amsterdam, North Holland.

Shaheed, Z. 1993. "Minimum wages and their impact on poverty", mimeo. Geneva, ILO.

Stewart, F. 1985. *Planning to meet basic needs*. London, Macmillan.

—. 1993. *War and underdevelopment: Can economic analysis help reduce the costs?*. Development Studies Working Paper No. 56. Oxford, International Development Centre.

Streeten, P.; Burki, S. J.; Ul Haq, M.; Hicks, N.; Stewart, F. 1981. *First things first: Meeting basic needs in developing countries*. New York, Oxford University Press.

United Nations Development Programme. 1993. *Human Development Report 1993*. New York, United Nations.

Weisbrod, B. A. 1969. "Collective action and the distribution of income: A collective approach", in US Congress, Joint Economic Committee: *The analysis and evaluation of public expenditures*. Washington, DC.

World Bank. 1986. *Poverty and hunger: Issues and options for food security in developing countries*. Washington, DC.

—. 1992. *India: Stabilizing and reforming the economy*. Washington, DC.

—. 1993. *World Development Report 1993 (Investing in health)*. Washington, DC.

5   Minimum wages and poverty

Zafar Shaheed[1]

I.   Introduction

In approaching the issue of minimum wages (MW) and poverty, two themes underlie this chapter. First, that wages in general, and minimum wages in particular, are clearly only part of a configuration of policies that need to be exploited in attacking poverty. Secondly, that, as far as minimum wage policy and poverty are concerned, there is not much new to discover in terms of principles, but there is perhaps some scope in terms of reinforcing the application of these principles, and combining MW policy with other anti-poverty policies. The chapter begins by noting the ILO standards governing minimum wage-fixing (MWF), discusses some of the objectives of the latter process and then moves on to some ideas about the place of minimum wage policy in a wider anti-poverty strategy.

II.   Minimum wage standards

ILO policy regarding remuneration is covered by three sets of international labour standards, supplemented by a few others not specifically dedicated to pay but which affect it, notably those governing freedom of association and the right to bargain collectively.[2] ILO instruments relating to MWF do not mandate the level of MWs as such, but rather the procedure for arriving at their level.[3] Particular emphasis is given to the need to associate employers and workers concerned in the

---

[1] International Labour Office, Geneva.

[2] For an exposition of these standards, see Starr & Swepston [1990].

[3] There is one exception to this rule, namely the Wages, Hours of Work and Manning (Sea) Convention (Revised), 1958 (No. 109), which provides that basic wages for seafarers will not be less than a specified amount.

operation of MWF machinery. The first ILO instrument relating to MWF (the Minimum Wage-fixing Convention, 1928 (No. 26)) has implicit in it the notion that, in the absence of satisfactory methods of pay determination, such statutory intervention becomes a substitute for collective bargaining. Also implicit is the hope that in time adequate collective bargaining machinery will develop in most of the economic sectors, thereby allowing for the withdrawal of such statutory intervention.

By 1970, when the more recent Minimum Wage-Fixing Convention (No. 131) — with special reference to developing countries — was adopted, it was evident that collective bargaining or other non-statutory means of wage determination were not spreading as widely and rapidly as might have been expected. Therefore, this Convention, adopted with special reference to developing countries, is more ambitious, requiring that MWF cover "all wage earners whose terms of employment are such that coverage would be appropriate." With its accompanying Recommendation No. 135, Convention No. 131 provides a little more guidance in addressing the question of the basis on which the MW should be set in each national context. Article 3 of this Convention requires that the MWF authorities take into account the following elements:

(i) the needs of the workers and their families, taking into account the general level of wages in the country, the cost of living, social security benefits, and the relative living standards of other social groups;

(ii) economic factors, including the requirements of economic development, levels of productivity, and the desirability of attaining and maintaining a high level of employment.

These elements provide an indication not only of the factors that should be taken into consideration in MWF, but also of some of the accompanying policies in combating poverty. As compared to the earlier, arguably more voluntarist, approach of Convention No. 26, Convention No. 131 and Recommendation No. 135 provide greater guidance to ratifying states, requiring them to broaden the scope of coverage, to fix and adjust MWs on a realistic, factual and analytical basis, to ensure the enforcement of MWs and, perhaps most importantly, to promote MWF as part of a national programme to overcome low pay and poverty. Against this brief description of selected aspects of the standards relating to MWs, we first consider the social and economic objectives of MWs, before seeing how these are related to the question of poverty alleviation.

III. Objectives of minimum wages

The minimum wage has been promoted as a policy instrument for poverty alleviation, by minimizing the scope for exploiting labour through bidding down of wages. Its ability to play such a role, by itself, will depend on the level and coverage of MWs, and upon ensuring compliance.

The question of coverage is crucial. The proportion of the workforce directly affected by the MW varies from country to country and depends partly on the basic role that governments assign to MWF. Most critics of MWs do not differentiate between these different roles and their associated economic consequences.[4] It is therefore necessary to consider these roles before proceeding further. Roles of MWF can be distinguished according to whether the machinery seeks to cover particular industries or occupations or, more broadly, all workers in general or all those within broadly defined sectors. Whether they are industry minimum wage systems or general minimum wage systems, they can affect a greater or lesser proportion of the workforce, and have a more or less ambitious role in terms of affecting general wage levels.

IV. Different roles, depending on scope

Under industry minimum wages, if the role is to use MWF to protect a relatively small number of workers in low-wage industries who occupy a specially vulnerable position in the labour market — the original role of the Wages Council system of the United Kingdom — government intervention is confined, so to say, to the bare minimum. It could be argued that this approach is thereby subject to less criticism from those who advocate policies based on "market forces". (However, this has not prevented the Government in the United Kingdom from abolishing the Wages Councils as of 1993.)

If the role is to fix wages for particular industries and/or groups of workers, going beyond the low-paid and unorganized, there is greater likelihood in principle of according a more ambitious role for MWF. Underlying this second role is the concept of ensuring "fair" wages, of establishing a "common rule" for individual industries or occupations in

---

[4] The most comprehensive discussion of the issues involved in minimum wage regulation is in Starr [1981]. For a recent survey of the law and practice relating to minimum wages, see ILO [1992].

order to promote the application of equal pay for equal work and to reduce areas of industrial conflict. There is also at least implicit in this approach, the desire to isolate wages from excessive competitive pressures, the rationale being that, while employers should be free to compete in terms of price, design, quality of product or service, it is unfair for competition to be based upon a bidding down of workers' wages.

There are in practice many problems with this approach to MWF, particularly prevalent in a number of developing countries influenced by the United Kingdom Wages Councils system. The more selective the coverage, the greater the difficulty to explain why some are covered and others not. The more comprehensive and detailed the occupational distinctions, the greater the administrative burdens. This has meant that in many countries, even though a comprehensive approach has been the stated objective, relatively few rates have been established and regularly adjusted. Therefore, despite the potentially far-reaching role of this "fair" wages approach, in practice this form of MWF by industry has tended not to have as great an effect as might be imagined.

Under systems providing for general minimum wages, one role can be to establish a general floor for the wage structure. This "safety-net" minimum, while generally applicable, frequently has direct relevance to only a minority of workers, as many are paid higher rates. This approach coincides with the view that a general minimum wage can make a contribution to reducing poverty only if it directly affects a relatively small proportion of the workforce. If a large proportion of workers received increases in money wages from the general minimum it is believed that subsequent inflation would not lead to any improvement in real wages, and/or that employment would be adversely affected (see the discussion below on selected Latin American countries).

The second role for general minimum wages is as an instrument of macro-economic policy, altering general wage levels and structures in line with broad national objectives of economic stabilization, growth and income distribution. This role assumes that the level and changes in minimum wages affect a large proportion of workers. It is seen as providing government with opportunities to apply more effective control over wage movements without adversely affecting resource utilization and allocation. However, this requires the wage fixing authorities to deal with a number of complex and difficult national economic and social issues simultaneously. The economic effects of changes in wages affecting a large proportion of the workforce, particularly the indirect effects, are uncertain and difficult to anticipate. This is especially true if much economic activity is strongly influenced by the terms of trade and changes at the international level over which the individual economy has no control. This helps to explain in large part why countries have tended to move away from this ambitious role of general minimum wages.

V. Effects on wages and employment

According to one view, particularly in periods of economic difficulty when activity in the formal sector is contracting, the existence of minimum wages exacerbates the adverse impact on employment. As demand declines, there is no possibility of employees keeping their jobs through adjustment of wage levels. Instead, they are dismissed and swell the ranks of the unemployed or the informal sector, which in turn forces wages down in this sector where minimum wages cannot be enforced. According to this view, those who remain employed in the formal sector thus protect their wages at the cost of increasing unemployment and depressing the living standards of informal sector workers, many of whom are already poor. Thus, for the economy as a whole, wage dispersion and inequality increase. However, within the formal sector, wage differentials between the skilled and unskilled are reduced and thereby also the incentive to accumulate human capital.

But it is easier to make assumptions in this area than to present hard evidence to support the assumptions. To engender the harmful consequences postulated by this traditional view, minimum wage levels would have to meet the following set of conditions: (i) exceed the wage levels that market forces would generate and thus represent a "binding" constraint on employers; (ii) apply to a large proportion of the workforce; and/or (iii) have a significant and positive impact on all wage levels in the formal sector; and (iv) have a negative impact on employment in the formal sector.

As regards the first point, there are some cases where minimum wages may have been relatively high in the past and a potential cause of labour market distortions. In some developing countries, high expectations in the post-colonial euphoria sometimes led governments to accord too ambitious a role to MWF. However, over the past 10 to 20 years, real minimum wages have decreased in many developing countries (see Table 1). In the more extreme cases where countries are suffering from wide discrepancies between official and "free" exchange rates, minimum wage payments are all but worthless.

The accuracy of the claims made about distorting effects of minimum wages will depend not only upon the direct coverage of minimum wages,

Table 1: Real index of minimum wages for selected countries (1980 = 100)

Country	1970	1971	1972	1973	1974	1975	1976	1977	1978	1979	1980
LATIN AMERICA											
Argentina	182.16	194.81	172.98	202.53	248.37	185.37	96.30	92.29	91.55	85.31	100.00
Bolivia	98.77	95.25	89.43	75.04	128.37	129.71	146.46	171.78	155.66	180.37	–
Brazil	90.41	90.55	92.64	96.46	90.05	94.61	95.55	95.80	97.91	97.52	100.00
Chile	64.24	71.65	62.70	48.35	60.25	60.89	67.50	79.63	100.64	99.83	100.00
Colombia	76.61	70.25	64.68	53.56	43.10	77.58	74.20	76.24	85.07	97.30	100.00
Costa Rica	87.67	91.12	89.44	83.68	77.66	77.26	84.36	89.92	96.84	99.17	100.00
Ecuador	49.09	56.61	52.48	46.43	50.20	50.79	58.98	52.19	46.75	56.52	100.00
Guatemala	118.44	118.98	118.35	106.22	108.28	95.68	86.42	76.93	71.05	63.81	100.00
Honduras	–	–	–	–	131.96	121.76	116.09	107.06	103.19	108.51	100.00
Mexico	90.77	86.23	97.52	87.04	101.52	90.76	109.13	114.48	109.94	106.98	100.00
Nicaragua	–	–	130.14	109.39	111.83	118.75	122.55	124.70	126.17	118.83	100.00
Panama	118.94	116.70	138.73	129.83	119.18	115.60	111.21	106.33	102.04	100.30	100.00
Paraguay	150.94	153.64	144.61	162.87	144.57	139.62	133.53	122.17	127.03	99.04	100.00
Peru	118.13	117.76	123.42	121.59	123.52	114.65	105.59	92.75	78.04	79.99	100.00
Uruguay	124.44	159.28	142.21	147.16	149.16	142.68	131.31	113.16	118.53	104.76	100.00
Venezuela	–	–	–	–	93.54	84.82	78.84	73.14	68.31	66.85	100.00
ASIA											
Philippines	101.43	94.40	87.25	74.84	61.57	65.31	72.49	78.37	79.81	88.35	100.00
Sri Lanka	72.57	75.06	72.63	72.88	76.25	83.94	90.36	91.20	98.30	103.69	100.00
Thailand	–	–	–	52.91	60.30	84.18	80.83	77.37	86.06	95.00	100.00

Table 1 (contd.): Real index of minimum wages for selected countries (1980 = 100)

Country	1970	1971	1972	1973	1974	1975	1976	1977	1978	1979	1980
AFRICA											
Algeria	56.26	56.91	65.00	65.78	75.52	69.31	73.45	69.89	83.88	88.01	100.00
Benin	–	–	173.68	164.07	139.68	143.11	125.68	118.04	108.89	99.45	100.00
Botswana	–	–	–	–	–	84.51	75.64	81.16	87.56	94.04	100.00
Burkina Faso	78.86	77.27	80.24	81.13	96.02	86.86	135.95	111.76	103.22	112.20	100.00
Congo	–	127.70	116.34	112.40	181.37	156.69	146.14	128.18	115.97	107.27	100.00
Côte d'Ivoire	103.76	105.37	105.02	104.49	121.90	114.07	127.23	99.87	110.46	104.20	100.00
Gabon	89.94	88.14	89.23	91.89	133.26	107.21	89.21	102.99	92.98	97.05	100.00
Ghana	415.08	378.86	458.95	389.98	660.24	508.56	325.83	225.80	173.94	112.62	100.00
Kenya	118.92	114.59	108.27	99.08	115.34	121.03	108.60	94.58	94.36	87.39	100.00
Malawi	–	–	–	–	–	119.46	108.32	96.53	95.70	93.58	100.00
Mauritius	–	–	–	–	–	–	125.60	127.13	126.19	119.05	100.00
Morocco	–	–	102.35	99.10	100.60	98.38	94.87	92.89	84.66	93.78	100.00
Niger	–	–	–	61.47	77.29	87.18	70.57	65.38	81.99	76.44	100.00
Senegal	98.86	95.17	89.65	92.64	146.16	111.02	109.83	98.64	95.38	86.98	100.00
Togo	142.78	147.63	137.04	132.26	128.88	131.10	117.43	110.28	96.61	97.06	100.00
Tunisia	–	67.69	66.30	63.37	76.00	77.37	73.45	91.64	96.61	97.06	100.00
Zaire	805.31	914.52	867.88	750.49	579.66	599.34	398.59	269.62	207.68	138.01	100.00

Table 1 (contd.): Real index of minimum wages for selected countries (1980 = 100)

Country	1980	1981	1982	1983	1984	1985	1986	1987	1988	1989	1990
LATIN AMERICA											
Argentina	100.00	97.78	103.56	152.91	167.50	113.06	110.00	120.79	93.56	42.05	50.20
Bolivia	–	–	166.04	100.00	82.23	33.21	30.83	35.66	37.22	33.77	31.20
Brazil	100.00	98.70	99.24	87.91	81.22	83.90	81.79	64.73	63.24	68.47	50.80
Chile	100.00	99.17	97.16	78.26	66.89	63.44	61.32	57.56	58.78	63.51	87.92
Colombia	100.00	97.21	101.47	105.89	111.23	107.60	112.24	111.06	108.36	109.37	106.71
Costa Rica	100.00	90.41	85.73	99.33	104.39	112.15	118.56	118.11	114.95	119.70	120.80
Ecuador	100.00	85.92	75.75	63.48	62.60	60.65	65.26	61.63	53.29	43.52	–
Guatemala	100.00	108.78	108.44	103.73	100.32	84.52	61.73	54.95	68.18	61.21	–
Honduras	100.00	105.72	105.82	97.76	93.34	90.31	86.54	84.44	80.81	73.56	–
Mexico	100.00	100.71	88.72	73.56	68.26	67.06	60.58	56.30	49.31	46.89	42.00
Nicaragua	100.00	91.87	78.08	59.57	66.76	47.32	–	–	–	–	–
Panama	100.00	93.19	89.39	102.09	101.82	100.79	100.85	99.86	99.61	99.62	99.00
Paraguay	100.00	–	–	–	–	–	–	–	–	–	–
Peru	100.00	57.96	77.56	79.32	61.68	54.17	55.77	60.16	45.48	24.21	21.40
Uruguay	100.00	103.30	104.62	89.65	89.84	94.13	89.26	91.20	84.94	78.57	69.00
Venezuela	100.00	86.08	78.53	73.89	65.88	95.29	90.91	110.91	92.80	77.11	65.20
ASIA											
Philippines	100.00	101.21	93.17	100.70	85.80	82.08	81.46	79.63	84.81	86.66	83.20
Sri Lanka	100.00	94.57	94.08	88.83	88.61	93.91	93.22	97.60	93.81	91.64	–
Thailand	100.00	108.48	110.20	110.98	112.58	116.57	114.46	115.30	112.16	110.84	117.43

Table 1 (contd.): Real index of minimum wages for selected countries (1980 = 100)

Country	1980	1981	1982	1983	1984	1985	1986	1987	1988	1989	1990
AFRICA											
Algeria	100.00	87.26	81.79	85.00	78.62	–	–	–	–	–	–
Benin	100.00	85.84	69.92	81.38	95.40	91.17	87.75	–	–	–	–
Botswana	100.00	106.63	106.60	110.96	113.12	112.52	114.59	115.71	114.12	116.21	–
Burkina Faso	100.00	92.98	105.09	97.00	92.52	86.54	88.86	91.46	100.40	100.89	101.40
Congo	100.00	85.50	75.77	70.29	85.37	95.93	93.63	91.57	88.32	–	–
Côte d'Ivoire	100.00	91.89	94.17	88.94	85.28	83.73	78.04	77.71	72.61	–	–
Gabon	100.00	91.99	90.88	83.31	89.04	89.89	86.67	87.57	97.05	90.71	83.54
Ghana	100.00	103.99	85.03	69.15	119.51	144.46	149.11	144.56	110.05	122.46	114.41
Kenya	100.00	89.43	78.20	70.12	63.64	67.55	64.99	68.67	–	–	–
Malawi	100.00	139.05	146.71	129.21	107.60	120.15	117.00	93.49	–	121.36	–
Mauritius	100.00	100.93	97.89	99.72	98.14	104.28	107.81	123.50	113.13	115.37	–
Morocco	100.00	100.97	106.69	113.78	111.92	117.89	115.28	112.25	120.53	128.50	131.89
Niger	100.00	81.36	72.87	74.73	68.97	69.61	71.92	77.09	78.18	80.44	81.10
Senegal	100.00	99.14	91.40	94.25	84.32	78.35	73.78	76.97	78.40	78.05	77.80
Togo	100.00	–	82.69	75.61	78.38	79.83	76.66	80.45	80.57	81.26	80.44
Tunisia	100.00	108.57	125.57	128.78	118.76	109.96	109.43	107.18	105.54	100.89	100.38
Zaire	100.00	76.17	63.23	91.26	162.45	163.96	–	–	–	–	–

Source: Anker et al. [1992]

but also upon their indirect impact on all wages. For example, if the minimum wage is increased it might be presumed that all those below the new minimum will either receive wage increases or become unemployed. There is also the possibility that other workers will receive increases in wages in order to maintain differentials or perhaps because the announcement of an increase in minimum wages has become the occasion on which to grant increases to others.

The effects of the minimum wage on wages actually paid are usually far from obvious, and can only be established after much detailed empirical analysis. The actual impact will depend greatly on the level of MWs relative to the previously existing pattern of wages. To estimate the costs of raising wages which were originally below the MW requires detailed information on the distribution of wages. This is much less readily available than data on average wage rates or earnings figures. Such data and research will help us to move away from the assumption of simplistic negative relationships between rising minimum wage levels and declining employment.

Detailed work in this area has been carried out in isolated instances, more in the developed than in developing countries. A recent workshop examined a number of such studies, and the general consensus seemed to be that the MW has at best a modest or no impact on employment.[5] Where it does have an effect, it is mostly on the employment of young workers and here, too, the findings are none too robust. However, there are also indications that too low a MW might have a negative effect in terms of labour supply. A study of the fast food industry in New Jersey, the United States found that, after an increase in the State MW, employment rose in fast food restaurants — an industry where many employees are close to the MW — suggesting that when the MW level is too low, workers can restrain their labour market activity [Card & Krueger, 1993]. Among developed economies, the United States is rather exceptional in terms of the low levels hit by its MW. In 1988, just over 4 per cent of the labour force was paid at the hourly MW prevailing at the time (US$3.35) [United States Department of Labor, 1990]. However, such low levels are far more common in developing countries, and lead one to question the effect of low MWs in continuing to provide any incentive for the poor to participate in wage employment in the labour force, which is an important function of wages.

---

[5] See papers presented at the International Workshop on the Economic Analysis of Low Pay and the Effects of the Minimum Wage (Arles, 30 Sept.-10 Oct. 1993), published in *International Journal of Manpower*, Bradford, 1994, Vol. 15, No. 2/3.

While studies on employment effects of MW are rare in developing countries, an earlier World Bank study of the Greater Santiago area in Chile produced findings not dissimilar from those noted in developed economies. The study, while ideologically critical of the MW, concluded that the MW was not necessarily "bad" and that more applied research was required to determine the groups most affected. It suggested that the only policy implications that could be made on the basis of the study at that stage might be "that MWs should not apply to young workers, or possibly to apprentices". The study also emphasized the importance of training to increase the human capital stock in the labour force, in order to reduce the population potentially covered by the MW [Riveros & Paredes, 1988].

Perhaps underlying the above statement is the argument made in the World Bank *World Development Report*, 1987, namely that minimum wage provisions reduce the differentials between skilled and unskilled workers, thereby reducing incentives for education and training. Any disincentive effect would be confined to those skills and occupations which are within the range of job and training choices of the unskilled workers or those affected by the MW provisions. It is extremely unlikely that individuals decide not to acquire university education and skills appropriate for entry to occupations such as engineers, accountants or doctors because there has been some narrowing of differentials between the MW and the salaries of these professions. As regards the question of whether any narrowing of wage differentials due to the MW would affect the decisions of individuals to undertake training appropriate to semi-skilled or skilled manual jobs, much might depend on who pays for the training and skill acquisition, and on the rewards for acquiring these skills. The more that training is provided, for instance, by employers through on-the-job training within internal labour markets, or by governments through well-established institutions within a coherent policy framework of recognizing, rewarding and utilizing the enhanced skills in appropriate ways, the less disincentive effect might be expected.

VI. MWs and the informal sector

It is necessary, on the subject of level and coverage of the MW, to address the question of whether MWs increase inequalities between the formal and the informal sectors, since this would have a negative effect on poverty and thereby argue against the usefulness of the MW in any poverty alleviation programme. This could happen if a rise in the MW led to a reduction in the employment of those covered by it and that this in turn increased the supply of labour in the informal sector, thereby driving down wages there. The converse case would be that a reduction of real wages in the formal sector (due in part to a reduction or removal of statutory MWs in that sector) would lead to shifts from informal to formal sector activity, but this would occur only if demand elasticities were high enough. Such assertions require empirical testing, and while there are various economic models that suggest these patterns, there is little supporting evidence.

One of the rare empirical studies of minimum wage regulations as they are given effect in the so-called informal sector resulted in some interesting findings. Carried out by the OECD Development Centre, covering 2,200 micro-enterprises in Algeria, Ecuador, Jamaica, Niger, Swaziland, Thailand and Tunisia, the first noteworthy finding of this study was that, contrary to common belief, the micro-enterprises in all seven countries are in principle not exempted from MW regulations. Equally contrary to expectations, it was found that most enterprises respect the law (with the exception of Niger and Swaziland, the poorest countries in the sample). However, employees tend to work longer hours than provided for in the law relating to hours of work, and are often not paid for this extra work. On the other hand, employers also responded that they often provide other benefits not included in the calculation of the wage rate (e.g. food, lodging, holiday bonuses, and annual transport home to rural areas). But perhaps the most interesting response of the employers to the survey was that MW legislation did not provide obstacles for micro-enterprises, that were more concerned by financial constraints, lack of demand for their products or services, taxes or — more rarely — other labour regulations. The study suggests that perhaps in view of high unemployment in the urban areas of the countries in the sample, de facto the authorities may have abstained from policing too closely regulations relating to MWs or working hours, whereas they manage to maintain respect for laws on taxes or hygiene standards in food outlets. It concludes by suggesting that by maintaining the MW at slightly higher levels than the equilibrium wage, the MW can probably help to improve the situation of employees of micro-enterprises [Morrisson, 1993].

VII. Other effects of the MW

In addition to preventing uncontrolled competition at the expense of labour, an important function of the MW is that it is supposed to encourage innovation and enhance productivity of labour. Underlying this role is the argument that, in the long run, competitive advantage of individual firms will depend on product competition, requiring an emphasis on research and development and product design and quality. Any low-pay strategy cutting the price of labour and trying to maintain profitability of increasingly obsolete equipment and product lines will eventually fail. In contrast to the orthodox economist's argument that low pay results from low productivity, there are circumstances in which low productivity results from low pay. For example, when sweatshop conditions, safety and health hazards and stress associated with the absence of any effective floor on pay and other conditions of employment or of employees' representation are directly detrimental to the health and well-being of workers, it can be argued that low pay and other related conditions of employment lead to lower productivity. This situation has been described as undervaluation of labour, fixing the value of labour below the real value of labour input [Wilkinson, 1994].

As hinted above, MWs, depending at which level they are set and/or maintained, help to keep wages down, paradoxical as this might sound. This is contrary to the orthodox contention that MWs tend to push up wages at all levels. In the absence of a statutory floor for MWs, it can be argued that MWs could in fact be higher in certain industries, leading to greater inequality of earnings. When MW rates are not adjusted systematically, they may provide a lag effect to other wage rates in the economy. This is illustrated by the case of Brazil, where the system of expressing wage-brackets for various groups as a multiple of the MW should in principle render the impact of changes in the MW rate greater than the coverage of the MW. Nevertheless, a study of the effects of changes in MWs in Rio de Janeiro suggests that about half the percentage changes in MWs are passed through to median wages. Thus, while a rise of 10 per cent in the real MW would lead to an increase of 4.8 per cent in median real wages, so also a fall in the value of the real MW leads to a fall in median real wages in Rio de Janeiro [Camargo, 1988]. A World Bank analysis of six other Latin American countries found no indication that MWs change the overall wage structure [Paldam & Riveros, 1987].

There is some fragmentary evidence from South Asia that, even though occupational MW rates are supposed to be minima and sometimes only recommendations, they are often taken as the final word regarding pay determination. Employers may be tempted, in the absence or weakness of collective bargaining, to use such minima, associated with job titles, as de facto maximum wage rates. Since they often tend to be adjusted only irregularly, such occupational minima can therefore contribute to an inertia on the part of certain employers in reviewing and revising upward levels of pay of specific occupations in line with changes in job content and skill enhancement. In these circumstances, MWF can be said to exert a lag effect on wage levels and perhaps on wage differentials.[6]

In different circumstances, the MW has been used effectively to hold down the wages of larger groups of employees. The pay of public sector employees (in so-called "budgetary" organizations) in Central and Eastern Europe is linked to the MW. In Russia, for instance, starting pay of the scale in budget organizations corresponds to the minimum wage. The amount paid to other employees is determined by multiplying the minimum rate by the coefficient provided for each respective category in the pay and grading structure. Because of this link to the MW, public sector employees are disadvantaged in comparison to those in the production sector. In March 1993, the national monthly average wage was 22,000 roubles, whereas the maximum possible salary at the top of the scale in the budgetary sector was 22,657 roubles per month. Similarly in Poland, the government used the MW to restrain public sector pay, where the average wage dropped by 30 per cent between 1990 and 1993, in comparison to the national average [Vaughan-Whitehead, 1993].

The MW can provide the basis on which social transfers are determined, thereby providing an important index for the national system of social protection. Its use as an anchor for such social protection has been particularly important in Central and Eastern Europe, and has led to a number of problems. Social benefits (e.g. unemployment benefits, pensions, education grants and children's allowances) are linked to the MW in these countries. The link with the MW was effectively a means for policy-makers to control social public expenditure, which has in turn led to arguments for de-linking the MW from such social protection. However, it is also argued that this would mean that the income of the poorest would be linked only to a few basic items (those normally kept under official control in such developing countries), leading to greater vulnerability of those with the poorest incomes. Nevertheless, given the low levels reached by the MW and by social benefits, and the reluctance of policy-makers to make increases in either as long as they remain linked, the argument for de-linking seems more compelling, associated with a policy of linking the MW with some index of cost-of-living. In this case, care will need to be given to ensuring some means of maintaining the purchasing power not only of MWs but also of social benefits [Vaughan-Whitehead, op. cit].

---

[6] For examples from the banking industry in India and Sri Lanka see ILO [1988, pp. 37-49 and pp. 185-195].

Finally, in listing some of the effects of MWs, mention should be made of the tripartite nature of MWF procedures in many countries. If properly maintained and adapted to national conditions, the tripartite consultations that characterize MWF institutions may have much to offer in terms of being a locus of dialogue and consensus building. Furthermore, they may have much to offer in helping to move towards some type of collective bargaining where this does not exist or is not effective. The problem, of course, is that it is already difficult to ensure the effective participation of organized employers' and workers' representatives in these bodies. How conceivably can the representatives of poorer, unorganized groups of workers be associated with these tripartite procedures?

MWF clearly needs to be coordinated with a variety of other policies in any attempt to address poverty issues. In addition to policies such as those relating to training, social transfers and prices, MWF policy also needs to be coordinated with the deployment of more macro-economic instruments, such as fiscal, monetary and trade policies. MWF plays a small role in this configuration, but the point is that a minimum attempt at some coordination is essential. While this is an area where it is difficult to marshal data and assert meaningful correlations, a PREALC analysis by Camargo and Garcia of a number of Latin American countries provides some insights into the role of MW policy associated with other interventions, in addressing poverty.[7]

VIII. Stabilization, MWs and poverty in Latin America

While most countries in Latin America experienced reductions in real MWs during the last two decades, as indicated in Table 1, Colombia and Costa Rica did not. It is interesting to look at the experience of these two countries, in comparison to two others with respectively rather different trends in their approaches to MW policy, used with other policy instruments, in addressing poverty.

Colombia and Costa Rica used a proactive minimum wage policy to establish a floor during the adjustment process, implying a policy of compression of the ratio between the average wage and the MW. In both countries, Camargo and Garcia argue that the MW contributed to a

---

[7] Camargo & Garcia [1993]. The following paragraphs on Chile, Colombia, Costa Rica and Guatemala are based on this study.

significant price deceleration during 1984-86 in Colombia, and during 1984-89 in Costa Rica.

Colombia implemented an active MW policy in the period 1982-88. During 1980-84, despite a growth in the fiscal deficit, external trade imbalances and a slow-down in growth, a deliberate policy of adjusting the MW annually *above* past inflation was pursued in a context of price deceleration. This latter condition was due to a fall in the real exchange rate (leading to formal devaluation in 1985) and a fall in food prices. Therefore, it is argued that in conditions of price deceleration, adjustment of the MW contributed to a real increase of the lowest wages and thereby contributed to poverty alleviation. However, during this same period, the unemployment rate increased. Was this due to an increase in the MW, or to other factors such as deceleration of growth and poor trade conditions, thereby affecting aggregate demand for labour? The increase of open unemployment during this period is noted to explain that the decrease in poverty — from 43.7 per cent in 1982 to 38.2 per cent in 1984 — during this period cannot be attributed to any growth in employment, but rather directly to increases in the wage income of poor families, determined by adjustments of the minimum wage. In 1985, when policies of devaluation and reduction of the external and fiscal deficit were implemented, the MW was reduced less than expected in relation to devaluation. Indeed, the loss in the real MW as a result of devaluation was overcompensated in 1986, after which it tapered off (see Table 2).

Table 2:   Evolution of the real minimum wage, 1980–1990
           (index 1980 = 100)

Year	Colombia	Costa Rica[1]	Costa Rica[2]	Chile	Guatemala
1980	100.0	100.0	100.0	100.0	100.0
1981	97.9	90.4	90.4	99.2	120.0
1982	102.7	84.1	85.8	97.2	120.7
1983	107.4	95.1	99.3	78.3	115.3
1984	112.7	100.1	104.4	66.9	111.4
1985	108.0	104.4	112.2	63.4	94.0
1986	113.9	106.6	118.5	61.3	68.6
1987	113.0	104.2	118.1	57.6	61.1
1988	108.5	100.8	115.0	61.7	75.9
1989	109.5	103.0	119.7	68.6	68.1
1990	105.7	104.0	120.8	73.3	48.2

Notes: [1] Average of the minimum wages. [2] Average of the lowest minimum wages.
Source: Elaborated by PREALC based on official data.

The adjustment programme led to growth and employment, and consequent reductions in unemployment. The devaluation did not lead to excessive price increases, since it was implemented in a series of unannounced mini-devaluations. A tripartite agreement was reached governing MW adjustments at a rate slightly higher than the inflation rate of the preceding year, thus establishing a base line for the evolution of real wages. Unemployment reduction, control of inflation, and the concerted MW adjustment policy are provided as *partial* reasons for maintaining poverty in 1988 at the same level as in 1984, despite the strong measures taken in fiscal and exchange rate policies. During the 1980s, there was also an increase in the proportion of active workers per poor household, which amplified the effect of the increase in the income of poor families.

However, in Colombia the absence of a sustained growth in *productivity* placed all the pressure of the increase of real wages on the inflation rate. In the longer term, the adjustment criterion of 100 per cent of past inflation contributed to slowly-increasing inflation.

Costa Rica also pursued a proactive MW policy designed to minimize the social costs of structural adjustment and stabilization policies, but was able to exploit its special system of multiple MW rates to adopt a more targeted approach. Full adjustments based on past inflation were applied only for the lowest income categories, so that the lowest MW rose by 20 per cent during 1980-89, whereas the MW corresponding to professionals was reduced by 27 per cent. Nominal readjustment was lower than past inflation for the average MW. An important aspect of MWF in Costa Rica is the tripartite negotiations within a national wages council, which contributes to a high degree of coordination between MW adjustments and other macro-economic policies. The Costa Rica case illustrates how a differentiated incomes policy can be used as an emergency instrument — during a limited period of time, it helped to protect the position of the lowest paid and provided a signal for inflation reduction by decreasing average MW. But it cannot be used as a systematic and permanent policy, as indicated by the dissatisfaction evinced by the middle and higher income groups towards the end of the 1980s.

In Chile and in Guatemala, in contrast to the above two cases, a fall in MWs contributed to an increase in poverty during adjustment periods. However, at the end of the 1980s and the beginning of the 1990s, Chile adopted a more systematic and active MW policy, with positive results on poverty.

In Chile, due to the inflation of 1973, MW adjustments were maintained below past inflation. However, since prices fell during 1974-81, an increase in real MWs occurred. Price deceleration was due in large part to a fall in the exchange rate plus an increase in productivity. During this period, collective bargaining was suspended and the MW was adjusted by administrative decision in the absence of any consultation. At the same time, the government recommended a full indexation of *average wages* to past inflation in the private sector. After the external shock to the economy experienced in 1982, the government de-indexed average wages from past inflation and maintained a MW policy designed to decrease inflation. This led to a drop of 40 per cent of the real MW between 1982 and 1987, with negative effects for poverty. In the pre-electoral period of 1988-89, however, an expansive MW policy was introduced, with adjustments greater than past inflation, in a situation of price deceleration. In 1990-92, Chile was able to increase real MWs in a context characterized by the following factors:

(i) a rapidly-growing economy, particularly the export sector;

(ii) a tight labour market with decreasing unemployment;

(iii) a deceleration of the inflation rate;

(iv) a sound supply of foreign exchange;

(v) high profit margins.

Equally important, however, is the fact that decisions on MW adjustments were taken together by the three social partners during this period. Finally, a new concept for adjustments was the agreement to use *expected* inflation plus average increase in productivity as the MW adjustment criteria. The net result, according to the authors, is that poverty was reduced from 40 to 33 per cent of households from 1990 to 1992 in Chile. The reasons for this decrease were growth of employment, increase in MW, rapid price deceleration, and an increase of activity rate within poor families.

The case of Guatemala is one of poor macro-economic management in general combined with an absence of concerted systematic efforts to adjust the MW, leading to a drop in the value of the real MW during the 1980s, so that by 1991 it was 38 per cent of its 1980 value. (In this respect, Guatemala is closer to many developing countries in Africa and some in Asia). During the first half of the decade, a recession in the external sector severely affected the level of economic activity, resulting in an important fall in exports during most of the decade. This was coupled with growing foreign debt. In 1981 the weight of foreign debt servicing represented 9 per cent of exports; this reached 44 per cent of exports in 1985. Two other elements of macro-economic policy affected growth (negatively) and poverty (positively) in Guatemala in this period: a significant drop in investment and the way in which the fiscal deficit was reduced. The latter was achieved through a reduction in social expenditure, without an increase in taxes. Finally, from 1981 to 1985, price stability was maintained largely as a result of a constant official exchange rate. However, as a result of the deterioration of the external accounts, a de facto devaluation took place in 1985, leading to a sharp increase in the consumer price index.

A new government, with the objectives of reducing inflationary pressures and improving the level of employment, governed from 1986 to 1989. However, inflation grew and open unemployment, which was 1.5 per cent in 1981, remained at around 6 per cent during this latter period. More significantly, the total proportion of the economically active population with "employment problems" (unemployed plus under-employed) is estimated to have risen to 54 per cent, while workers earning less than the MW rose to 55 per cent.

On the basis of these — and other PREALC — findings, Camargo and Garcia argue that for open economies in transition, combating inflation in particular as an important source of persistent poverty, MW policy should be designed to achieve the following objectives:

(i) signal a de-indexation from past inflation;[8]

(ii) induce adoption of incentives for increases in productivity and means of participating in its increase and its results;

(iii) contribute to the development of a social safety net, in association with unemployment insurance, family allowances and other social benefits;

(iv) strengthen the social dialogue.

Their final conclusions are that an increase in workers' welfare and a decrease in poverty are dependent on two major factors. The first is price deceleration which, in combination with appropriate MW adjustments and increases in productivity, leads to an increase in the real wages of lower income workers. The second is an increase in employment — or a decrease

---

[8] Camargo and Garcia propose using a criteria of expected inflation (Pe), to which average annual increase in productivity (q) is added to stimulate the adoption of corresponding initiatives. Therefore, they propose that MW adjustment = Pe + q. For cases where inflation is very high, they suggest using as transitional formula incorporating past (Pp) and expected (Pe) inflation, in which case MW adjustment = (a.Pp + b.Pe), where b = (1-a).

in unemployment — achieved by a MW policy that signals wage adjustment moderation. These are significant empirical findings to support some
of the assertions made about the important but partial role that MWF can
play in national programmes designed to alleviate poverty.

The question of compliance has been purposefully left until the end,
since it is in a sense the most crucial issue. Put somewhat brutally, the
MW tends to be applied and complied with mainly in those areas where it
is least required: large enterprises in the formal urban sector, where
workers tend to be better organized and enjoy collective bargaining rights
through which they tend to acquire pay and other conditions of employment well above the minimum. It is often argued that when MWs are set
too high relative to market conditions, this results in widespread non-
compliance and distortions across complying and non-complying enterprises. While there is ample evidence of non-compliance, and poorest
compliance in those areas where the poor tend to be concentrated (the
unorganized sector, small and medium-sized enterprises, the services
sector, to say nothing of rural areas), this is not a reason to abolish the
MW, or to provide differential rates. What is required, beyond the traditional appeals — necessary as they are — to strengthen the inspection and
enforcement function of government labour departments and to increase the
size of penalties (while retaining MWs at a level which is more feasible to
enforce) is an effort to find practical means of ensuring that workers have
the capacity and strength to report violations and to seek redress.

This has to start with the application of the right to organize and to
bargain collectively. But this is still limited to the organized and protected
minority of workers. How can the more impoverished groups of society be
accounted for in this process? The key point is to ensure organization and
representation of the poor, so that their organizations have a voice vis-à-vis
institutions like these for MWF. This is a daunting task, given the already
weak situation of MWF machinery as regards the representatives of the
organized employers and workers, and requires, inter alia, an introspection
on the part of the latter, as regards their continuing relevance in terms of
representation of broader social interests and their willingness and ability
to ally with and help to organize these broader elements of society.

IX. Concluding remarks and areas of further work

This chapter has attempted to provide arguments in support of the
contention that MWs do not necessarily have a negative effect on employment nor a positive one on wage levels, especially at the sort of levels they

have reached. Indeed, it may be argued that there is room in many cases for certain upward adjustments, which could have positive effects for the various employment, training and productivity issues raised, which in turn constitute long-term durable solutions for poverty alleviation.

To achieve this, intervention is required in the labour market to stop any further degradation of wages. This implies stronger political and administrative support for MWF systems, which presently suffer from inadequate participation by employers' and workers' representatives, lack of appropriate data and technical expertise, insufficient periodic adjustments of MW rates and, above all, poor enforcement machinery. But this is clearly not enough for combating poverty. In any poverty alleviation effort, labour market interventions, such as MWF, need to be combined with redistributive transfer programmes as well as with a realignment of macro-economic and governance policy stressing redistribution, equity and solidarity.

Much political, normative and research work is required to pursue these goals. Research is essential to provide empirical backing to principles which might otherwise come to be regarded as mere dogma. In this respect, the highly controversial and politicized debate on the economic effects of labour standards and regulations needs to be addressed. The "pessimists" in this debate argue that labour standards and regulations emanating from them are bad for growth and productivity, making workers undisciplined and resistant to change, constituting additional labour costs for employers, thereby limiting their flexibility and inducing inefficient recruitment and dismissal decisions. The "optimists" argue that such regulation has positive economic effects on productivity by inducing employment security, through which high returns can be achieved from both training and from workers' commitment to enterprise performance. They go so far as to argue that lengthening labour contracts and maintaining high costs of dismissals could induce employers to make higher investments in training, and lead to greater labour-management cooperation.

These arguments are far from conclusive, and require further work based on concrete research to ascertain the economic effects of labour standards and regulation on employment and productivity. This research would need to control for factors other than minimum wage and other labour regulations resulting in labour-saving production processes, e.g. technological progress, capacity utilization, work organization and rationalization, efficiency of management, and relative openness of the economy, to mention but a few relevant considerations [Rodgers & Figueiredo, 1993].

Bibliographical references

Anker, R. et al. 1992. "Minimum wages in developing countries: Trends and determinants", mimeo.

Camargo, J. M. 1988. "Minimum wages in Brazil: Theory, policy and empirical evidence", in ILO: *Assessing the impact of statutory minimum wages in developing countries*, LMR 67. Geneva, International Labour Office.

Camargo, J. M.; Garcia, N. B. 1993. *Stabilization, minimum wages and poverty*. Santiago, PREALC/ILO.

Card, D.; Krueger, A. 1993. "Minimum wages and employment: A case study of the fast food industry in New Jersey", paper presented at NBER Summer Institute, Cambridge, Ma., Harvard University, July.

ILO. 1988. *Technological change, work organization and pay: Lessons from Asia*. Geneva, International Labour Office.

—. 1992. *Minimum wages: wage-fixing machinery, application and supervision*. Geneva, International Labour Office.

Morrisson, C. 1993. "Le problème des bas salaires et du salaire minimum dans les pays en développement", paper presented at the International Conference on the Economic Analyses of Low Pay and the Effects of the Minimum Wage (Arles, 30 Sept.- 10 Oct. 1993).

Paldam, M.; Riveros, L. 1987. "The causal role of minimum wages in six Latin American labor markets", April (mimeo), quoted in Paukert, F.; Robinson, D. (eds.): *Incomes policies in a wider context: Wage, price and fiscal initiatives in developing countries*. Geneva, International Labour Office, 1992.

Rodgers, G. B.; Figueiredo, J. B. 1993. "Internal IILS report on a seminar on Labour institutions in the context of economic transformation in Latin America". Santiago, PREALC, May.

Starr, G. 1981. *Minimum wage fixing; an international review of practices and problems*. Geneva, International Labour Office.

Starr, G.; Swepston, L. 1990. "Remuneration and international labour standards", in *Bulletin of Comparative Labour Relations* (Deventer), No. 19, pp. 37-60.

United States Department of Labor. 1990. *Monthly Labor Review* (Washington, DC), Jan.

Vaughan-Whitehead, D. 1993. "Minimum wage in Central and Eastern Europe: Slippage of the anchor", paper presented at the International Conference on the Economic Analysis of Low Pay and the Effects of Minimum Wages (Arles, 30 Sept.-10 Oct. 1993).

Wilkinson, F. 1994. "Equality, efficiency and economic progress: The case for universally applied equitable standards for wages and conditions of work", in Sengenberger, W.; Campbell, D. (eds.): *Creating economic opportunities: The role of labour standards and labour institutions in industrial restructuring*. Geneva, International Institute for Labour Studies, pp. 61-68.

6 The feminization of poverty? Research and policy needs

Mayra Buvinić[1]

I. Introduction

Because women often start from disadvantaged positions... policy which does not specifically discriminate in favour of women ends up reinforcing gender inequality. This is notably true of many of the mechanisms which underlie poverty. While figures are difficult to come by, it is almost certain that a significantly higher percentage of women are poor than of men. [From "The framework of ILO action against poverty", prepared by an ILO working group, monograph 1, Chapter 1].

Are women in developing countries really less well-off than men? And, if this is so, what are the implications for policy and for policy-oriented research? This paper addresses these questions and therefore explores in more detail the statements made in the ILO paper quoted above. The paper uses empirical evidence to examine whether poverty in developing countries has, in fact, become feminized and discusses the possible underlying causes and consequences of women's poverty. It also reviews the related trend of the feminization of unpaid and low-paid work. The tentative conclusion is that the poverty of women differs from that of men in both degree and kind. Women appear to experience greater poverty than men and to transmit their disadvantage more readily to their children. Anti-poverty policies, therefore, need to — but do not yet — effectively reach poor women to minimize the poverty of this and the next generation. These policies need to be crafted to respond to the unique conditions of women in poverty. The paper ends with suggestions for the design of policies and a policy-oriented research agenda that should more effectively address the needs of women and children in poverty.

[1] International Center for Research on Women, Washington, DC. Paper prepared for International Institute for Labour Studies Poverty Symposium, 22-24 November 1993.

II. The feminization of poverty

The feminization of poverty, linked closely to the rise of poor households headed by women, is both an accepted and well-documented trend in the United States [Ross & Sawhill, 1976; Garfinkel & McLanahan, 1986]. The possibility that a similar trend may have occurred in developing countries is neither well-recognized nor accurately documented. For instance, the *World Development Report* on poverty is sympathetic to the plight of poor women, but concludes that there is not enough evidence to assert changes in the composition of poverty groups by sex, and only mentions in passing the large numbers of single-mother households among the poor [World Bank, 1990]. There is still a reluctance to acknowledge that women may be worse-off than men among the poor in developing countries, despite data on woman-headed households and estimates of rural poverty by sex that suggest that women's share of poverty in developing countries has grown more than that of men.

III. The poverty of rural women

The last decade has not been kind to the poor. The economic crisis of the early 1980s wiped out gains the developing countries had achieved in the 1970s in terms of improvements in living conditions. The recovery from the crisis has been slow at best. According to World Bank estimates, the head count index of poverty (that is, the estimated share of the population consuming less than $32 per person per month at 1985 purchasing power parity prices), as well as the numbers of poor people, rose between 1985 and 1990 in three regions: sub-Saharan Africa, the Middle East and North Africa, and Latin America and the Caribbean [World Bank, 1993]. In South Asia the share of the poor diminished but their absolute numbers increased, and only East Asia made gains in terms of reducing both the proportions and numbers of the poor. A recent IFAD study of the extent of rural poverty in developing countries, calculated on the basis of 41 countries with data which account for 84 per cent of the total rural population of 114 developing countries, indicates both growing numbers and proportions of women among the rural poor since the mid-1960s. Table 1, based on these estimates, shows that between 1965-70 and 1988 the number of rural women living below the poverty line rose more than the number of rural men living below the poverty line (47 per cent for women versus 30 per cent for men). That is, while in 1965-70 women comprised 57 per cent of the rural poor, by 1988 they accounted for 60 per cent [Jazairy et al., 1992].

Table 1:   Total number of rural people living below poverty line by sex
           (estimated in millions)

	1965-70[3]	1988[1]	Percentage Change[2]
Women	383,673	564,000	47.0
Men	288,832	375,481	30.0
Total	672,505	939,481	39.7

Notes: [1] Totals for 114 countries are given in Jaziry et al. [1992, Table 6 (pp. 404-5) and Table 13 (pp .422-23)].
           [2] Per cent changes are given in Jaziry et al. [1992, p.273] on the basis of 41 countries with data which
           account for 84 per cent of the total rural population of 114 developing countries.
           [3] Figures for 1965-70 were extrapolated using the 1988 totals and per cent changes.
Source: Jaziry et al. [1992].

IFAD's explanation for rural women's worsening poverty can be grouped into three categories. First, explicit gender biases in the allocation of productive services, such as rural credit, and productive resources, such as land allocations, that negatively affect women's rural productivity; second, a drop in agricultural production in sub-Saharan Africa and intensified degradation of the environment (related to population pressures) that lead to increases in women's work burdens; and third, family disintegration, male desertion, male migration and single motherhood that result in the formation of households headed by women and families maintained by women).

IV. The poverty of woman-headed households

IFAD found that the percentage of rural households headed by women was significant in two different regression models to explain the percentage of rural populations below the poverty line in different countries [Jazairy et al., 1992]. While comparable and reliable statistics for countries over time are not available, it is generally agreed that the percentage of households headed by women and of families maintained by women has risen in both developing and industrialized countries [Folbre, 1991]. In the former, the percentage of households headed by women varies from the mid-teens in some South and South-east Asian countries, to close to half of all households in some African and Caribbean countries, as shown in Table 2. Table 3 shows that the percentage of households headed by women has grown in five out of six Latin American countries that have compiled these statistics over time.

Table 2: Percentage of households headed by women in the 1980s (selected countries)

Botswana	45
Barbados	45
Jamaica[3]	42
Malawi	29
Cuba[1]	28
Ghana	27
Venezuela[1]	22
Honduras	22
Chile[2]	20
Bangladesh[1]	17
S. Korea[1]	15
Indonesia	14

Notes: [1] Folbre [1991]
            [2] CASEN. 1990. A survey of national socio-economic characteristics conducted by the Ministry of Planning
            in collaboration with the Department of Economics, University of Chile.
            [3] Louat et al. [1992]
Source: United Nations [1991].

Table 3: Trends in female headship in selected Latin American countries (in percentage)

Country	Year	Percentage
Brazil	1960	10.7[3]
	1970	13.0[1]
	1986	18.4[4]
Costa Rica	1982	17.0[1]
	1984	17.5[2]
Dominican Republic	1980	21.7[1]
	1987	26.1[1]
Honduras	1974	22.0[2]
	1986-1987	20.2[2]
Mexico	1977	13.6[1]
	1980	14.0[1]
Peru	1970	14.1[1]
	1981	22.0[1]

Sources: [1] Acosta, Felix [forthcoming].
            [2] García & Gomáriz [1989].
            [3] Merrick & Schmink [1983].
            [4] Barros et al. [1989].

Figure 1: Percentage of woman-headed households among all households in selected cities, by class

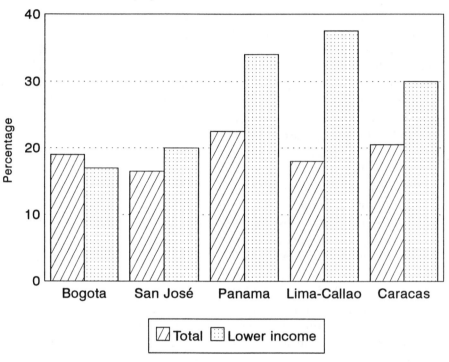

Source: United Nations [1984].

More important, a number of studies carried out in the last decade indicate that these households are over-represented among the poor. In a recent review of 60 empirical studies that examined the relationship of female headship to poverty, 44 established that female-headed households were poorer than male-headed households. These studies reached this conclusion by using a variety of poverty indicators, including total household income, per capita household income, mean income per adult equivalence, per capita consumption of expenditures, and ownership of land and assets, among others. Eight other studies found that poverty was associated with certain types of female heads, or that the association emerged for certain poverty indicators [Buvinić & Gupta, 1993]. Figure 1 presents data gathered in the mid-1980s for five cities in Latin America. The figure shows that, with the exception of Bogota — where there was a greater proportion of woman-headed households in the total population than among the lower income groups — woman-headed households were over-represented in the lower income groups in the other four cities examined.

The studies that show a relationship between female headship and poverty point to three sets of factors that determine the greater poverty of woman-headed households. First, woman-headed households, despite their smaller size in comparison to other types of households, often carry a higher dependency burden — a higher ratio of non-workers to workers — than do other households. This type of household composition would not necessarily lead to poverty if the household received child support payments from absent fathers (as is the case with some left-behind rural female heads in Africa who receive adequate remittances). The poverty of woman-headed households thus reflects a disruption of traditional systems of family governance that enforced income transfers from fathers to children [Folbre, 1991].

Second, the main earners of woman-headed families are, by definition, women who have lower average earnings than men, fewer assets and less access to remunerative jobs and productive resources such as land, capital and technology. This gender-related economic gap contributes to the economic disadvantage of woman-headed families. A recent analysis of wage differentials by sex in 15 Latin American countries shows that women are paid on average 70.5 per cent of what men are paid, and that differences in human capital explain only 20 per cent of the observed wage gap. The unexplained variability is presumably the result of discrimination [Psacharopoulos & Tzannatos, 1992]. An analysis of the earnings of household heads in Belo Horizonte, Brazil revealed that the less remunerative jobs open to women in the labour market (rather than sex disparities in education) explained most of the differentials in earnings between male and female heads. Fifty-three per cent of the female heads held low-paying jobs in the informal sector, but only 30 per cent of the male heads did so [Merrick & Schmink, 1983]. In rural areas of Botswana the mean yearly income, including, transfers is 903 Rand for male-headed households and only 433 Rand for female-headed ones. These rural households headed by women in Botswana are poorer than those headed by men, not because women are less educated than men, nor because they work less than men. They are poorer because they have less land, fewer oxen to use for ploughing and less access to other productive resources, such as farm technology and agricultural extension [Koussudji & Mueller, 1983].

Third, there may be an independent effect of female headship on household economic vulnerability that cannot be reduced to the characteristics of women or of the household. Women who are heads of households also have to fulfil home production and domestic roles. Therefore, they face greater time and mobility constraints than male heads, which can result in an apparent "preference" for working fewer hours for pay, for choosing lower-paying jobs that are more compatible with child care, and for spending more for certain services such as water and housing, because they cannot contribute time to offset transaction costs. Women who head households may also encounter discrimination in access to jobs or resources beyond that which they encounter because of their gender, or may make inappropriate choices that affect the household's economic welfare because of social or economic pressures. In Jamaica, despite the fact that renting housing is a more expensive long-term alternative than purchasing it, many women who head households remain renters, lacking access to assets and credit [McLeod, 1988]. Women farmers who head households in Botswana and Malawi cannot take up on- or off-farm income generation activities because of their heavy domestic and subsistence responsibilities [Kossoudji & Mueller, 1983; Chipande, 1987].

Lastly, female heads may have a history of premature parenthood and family instability that tends to perpetuate poverty to succeeding generations. Premature unpartnered parenthood is happening with increasing frequency in developing countries, especially in Latin America and in sub-Saharan Africa [Singh & Wulf, 1990; PRB, 1992], and studies indicate that early sexual experience and early childbearing, as well as low educational attainment and remaining unmarried, are key links in the intergenerational transmission of poverty between mothers and their children [Fürstenberg et al., 1987; Buvinić et al., 1992].

Research on the consequences of adolescent motherhood highlights an important distinction between families and households and indicates the dependency of female headship on access to housing. Sub-families maintained by women (mostly single mothers) within households rather than woman-headed households become prevalent when there are economic downturns, chronic housing shortages and/or where women, because of social customs or financial constraints, cannot set up independent housing. In 1990 slightly more than one in every five households in Santiago, Chile, where low-income housing shortages are chronic, accommodated a sub-family within it; more than half (50 per cent) of these sub-families were headed by single mothers. When these families are counted, the percentage of female headship in Santiago rises from 20.8 per cent of all households to 27.2 per cent of all families [Buvinić & Valenzuela, forthcoming]. Do sub-families share in the wealth of the household or do they depend on the single mother's income, and should they be counted as separate families to estimate the demand for services, such as housing? These are some of the questions that research on women in poverty needs to address.

V. Measuring family poverty

Sub-families signal the complexity of family forms and arrangements that hide behind or under the term household, and raise the question of the appropriate indicator or measures of household and family poverty, and the poverty of female headship. Visaria [1980], in an often-cited study, compared the economic status of woman-headed households in India using total household expenditures versus per capita expenditures. He found that woman-headed households were over-represented among the poor when using total household economic indicators, but that this did not hold true when using per capita measures. But Visaria did not disaggregate his sample by type of female headship, while female headship picks up families in a variety of situations and needs to be cross-tabulated by age and marital status of the head (to gauge origins) and presence of children (to assess dependency burdens) in order to more finely discriminate poverty conditions. Another study which concludes that the expectation that woman-headed households in Jamaica are highly correlated with poverty "can be put to rest" shares the problem of not disaggregating female heads with substantial dependency burdens from those with no children or other dependents to support [Louat et al., 1992].

More generally, per capita measures of household economic status, income or consumption, fail to capture different dependency ratios across headship types. As Lloyd and Brandon [1991] and Bruce and Lloyd [forthcoming] argue, there are two problems with using per capita consumption as a poverty indicator. First, this measure may underestimate consumption levels of male- when compared to female-headed households. Information on household consumption is generally gathered from one knowledgeable person in the household, generally the woman. In smaller households (and woman-maintained households tend to be smaller), the consumption is likely to be more visible. Moreover, since women in these households are more likely to be the chief earners, they are also likely to more accurately report household consumption than heads of larger households (male or female). This tends to inflate the consumption of the female-maintained smaller households and understate that of male-headed and larger households. Further, consumption expenditure measures may be substantially augmented by home-produced goods, especially in farm households — at the expense, however, of women's time spent in its production and a consequent decline in their ability to use time in income-generating activities.

In support of the hypothesis that consumption expenditure measures may be subject to gender biases, Lloyd and Brandon document the economic disadvantage of female-headed households in Ghana through other indicators. These households have less access to land, credit, and education; have higher dependency ratios; depend more on outside support; and work significantly longer hours. Rogers [1991] similarly found that female-headed households in the Dominican Republic, although not over-represented among the poor, were more economically vulnerable than male-headed households because of a greater dependence on income transfers in the form of gifts and remittances from others.

A last argument against using per capita expenditure measures is presented in a paper by Visaria [Visaria & Visaria, 1985]. Total household expenditures, they argue, is "a better indicator of the level of living compared to per capita expenditures, because household implies certain basic establishment costs, formation of assets, etc., some of which are more or less independent of the size of the household" [p. 83]. By using total household expenditures as the indicator, these authors found that female-headed households in India were concentrated in the lower expenditure groups. In addition, these households were more economically vulnerable than other types of households because female heads possessed little or no land, were less literate, and were burdened by the need to combine household work with earning a livelihood.

The weight of the evidence therefore, indicates that female-headed families with children to support tend to be disproportionately represented among the poor. Finding solutions to the poverty of female headship should be relatively straightforward if household composition factors are the main determinants of their poverty; it should be more complex if the interaction of headship and gender predominates. In the former case, policy-makers could be optimistic about targeting interventions that alleviate these households' dependency burden (such as income-generation programmes for adults of either sex who are supporting many dependents and cash transfers for these households). In the latter case, the policy interventions should include — in addition to expanding income-earning opportunities and providing child-care support — affirmative policies to prevent discrimination in access to markets and resources, aggressive health and education campaigns (and services for pregnant teenagers, for instance) and the establishment of effective social support networks through formal or informal organizations. In this latter case, targeting all women, with the expectation that female heads would benefit, would fall short in solving the disadvantages of female heads.

VI. The feminization of unpaid and low-paid work

1. Women's unpaid work

Time-use studies conducted in the past two decades indicate gender differences in the way poor families allocate labour (home and market production) and leisure, with the weight of extra work burdens falling on women:

1. Poor women tend to work longer hours and have less leisure time than poor men [Leslie, 1988].

2. When these working hours are assigned an economic value and added to the household's cash income, the contribution of poor women and children to household income can be greater than that of poor men [King & Evenson, 1983].

3. Unlike the evidence from industrialized societies which shows a trade-off between market work and child care, evidence from developing countries indicates that poor women tend not to make trade-offs between child care and market work. When these women enter the workforce, it is leisure time rather than home production time that is reduced [Popkin, 1983].

4. As in industrialized countries, women and children in developing countries must adapt to the differing demands of household and market, whereas men's roles remain resistant to change. Increasing household burdens such as additional children or declining household income, tend to change women's and children's but not men's allocation of time between home and market production and leisure [King & Evenson, 1983].

In summary, poor women in developing countries have both home and market production roles, and the poorer the household, the more burdensome and more important both roles become. While the conventional way is to divide time allocation into home and market production, child care, and leisure, recent studies have included the time women spend in unpaid community management work as a separate category [Moser, 1993; Commonwealth Secretariat, 1991]. These studies document growing time spent in community work in order to compensate for the decreasing provision of governmental services associated with structural adjustment programmes (SAPs). This female "added worker" effect is reflected in the community kitchens in Peru that were set up and run by poor women at the height of the economic crisis in the 1980s

[Francke, 1992] and the volunteer work of women to provide community services in Guayaquil, Ecuador [Moser, 1993].

The Guayaquil study followed women over a decade and revealed that the allocation, rather than the amount, of women's work time changed as the result of the cut-backs in government services associated with the SAP. Women increased time allocated to productive and community activities at the expense of reproductive activities, with costs for themselves and their children. The shift from non-tradables to tradables in African agriculture associated with SAPs may similarly have increased women's unpaid labour in men's farms, and decreased women's control over the returns of their labour [Palmer, 1991]. It is likely that poor women have compensated for the reduction in government health service delivery by increasing time spent in the provision of primary health care activities [Leslie et al., 1988].

This flexibility in the allocation of women's time to the multiple roles of home, market, community and health work in response to external demands on the family, such as those imposed by SAPs, is a unique gender feature in poor families, one that differentiates poor women from their better-off counterparts, and one that suggests key mechanisms and points for intervention in the transmission of poverty from mothers to children. The Guayaquil study reveals that women that are "coping" or "hanging on" in response to the additional work burdens imposed by SAP, are in stable partner relations or have female sources of support in the family. Women who instead are "burnt out" and unable to cope are most likely to be heads of household and have handed over reproductive responsibilities to older daughters who, therefore, have to drop out of school, insuring the perpetuation of poverty from one generation of women to another [Moser, 1993]. The analysis of African agriculture under SAPs predicts that the women's expanded work burdens could lead to a new crisis of poverty, keeping poor households in a high-mortality and high-fertility frame while agricultural incomes rise [Palmer, 1991].

2. Women's low-paid work

Two recent trends help to explain low-income women's growing participation in low-paid, unprotected and often uncounted work in developing countries. Evidence reveals that the worldwide economic crisis of the early 1980s motivated low-income women to seek paid work in order to compensate for real declines in household income. In addition, the outward-oriented export promotion policies that have been in vogue since the mid-1980s in a majority of countries in the South — as part or independent of SAPs — have increased the demand for women workers willing to work for low wages.

There are historical precedents for families' increased reliance on women's wages during economic recessions. During the Great Depression of 1929-32 in the United States, women secondary workers took up marginal and part-time jobs available while unemployed men searched for higher-wage jobs. The proportion of gainfully employed women rose, while the unemployment rate among women decreased and that of men increased during the height of the depression [Humphries, 1988]. A similar change was observed in industrialized countries during the 1974-75 world recession: female labour force participation rates increased in 11 out of 15 OECD countries and female unemployment declined [OECD, 1976].

Data on this "added worker" effect — that is, the voluntary entrance of females into the paid workforce to increase family income — is available for a number of Latin American countries in the 1970s and the 1980s. A common problem with the data is the separation of cyclical effects related to economic downturns from the secular rise in female labour participation rates that may confound the effects or prevent the rising trend from reverting back to its pre-recession stage at the end of the cycle. Data for Chile during the 1974-75 economic crisis is perhaps the clearest in illustrating the "added worker" effect of the recession without a confounding rising secular female participation trend. Despite a trend towards long-term declines in women's labour force participation, women's activity rates in the lowest quintiles of the household income distribution increased sharply, from 18 to 22.4 per cent. The reverse happened with women in the upper quintiles of the household income distribution, and both trends reverted back to their pre-crisis levels with the end of the recession, as Figure 2 reveals [Rosales, 1979]. Added worker effects for women in response to the economic downturns of the early 1980s have been documented for Argentina, Brazil, Costa Rica, Mexico and Uruguay [ICRW, 1992; Moser et al., 1993].

The economic downturns of the early 1980s increased the supply of women workers, while the outward-oriented economic policies that followed the recession increased the demand for female labour in unregulated manufacturing and agribusiness jobs that pay individual rather than family wages, often include subcontracting arrangements, and offer few or no benefits and no employment security. Table 4 reflects the feminization of work in developing countries, by indicating many more instances of countries where activity rates of women have increased rather than decreased in the 1980s as compared to the activity rates of men [Standing, 1989]. Table 5 indicates that, in many countries, women comprise almost half of the self-employed, a category that includes subcontracting and piece-work for export promotion industries as well as traditional, small-

Figure 2: Rates of female labour force participation in Chile by family income level for selected years (comparing peak recession (1975) with pre- and post-recession years)

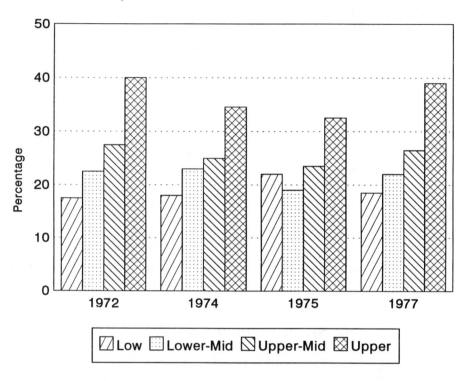

Source: Rosales [1979]

Table 4: Feminization of work in developing countries in the 1980s (activity rates)

	Type of change	Per cent
Women	Increased	69
	Decreased	8
	No change	22
	Total	99
Men	Increased	36
	Decreased	33
	No change	31
	Total	100

Source: Standing [1989]

**Table 5: Percentage of women in self-employed/unprotected work
(selected countries)**

AFRICA[1]	
Congo	(1984) 39
Gambia	(1983) 25
Zambia	(1986) 53
LATIN AMERICA	
Ecuador (Quito)[2]	(1985) 50
Mexico (Urban)*[3]	(1981) 35
Bolivia (La Paz)[4]	(1983) 48
ASIA	
India[5]	(1981) 49
Indonesia[1]	(1980) 43
Malaysia[1]	(1986) 43

Note: * excludes domestic servants.
Sources: [1] United Nations [1991, p. 93]. [2] Buvinić et al. [1989, p. 223]. [3] PREALC [1981]. [4] Casanovas et al. [1985, p. 217]. [5] Mitra [1981].

scale commercial and production activities linked to local rather than international markets.

VII. Consequences of women's poverty

The increasing numbers of poor families headed by women and the feminization of work at home and in the market go hand-in-hand. This can set in motion a vicious cycle of poverty and deprivation where poverty causes increased female work that, in turn, exacerbates women's and children's deprivation and poverty, unless women find work that pays adequately. Until fairly recently, the prevailing assumption was that any positive income effect of poor women's employment on children's health and well-being would be offset by negative effects of reduced child-care time by working mothers or by the substitution of older siblings in child care. Recent studies, however, do not support this assumption. Instead, they signal the importance of the productivity of women's work and the level of women's wages in insuring child nutrition. There is a negative effect of women's employment on child nutrition only if mothers work very long hours at sub-standard wages [Leslie, 1988]. Otherwise, there is no effect or, as the evidence below points out, a positive effect of women's paid work and control of income on child nutrition.

Investigations that use female headship, the proportion of household income women earn, or women's unearned income as proxies for women's control over income find significant positive effects of income in women's hands-on measures of child well-being, especially in the case of poor households. In Brazil, for instance, income in the hands of the mother has an effect on child health that is almost 20 times greater than income that is controlled by the father [Thomas, 1990]. In Guatemala it takes 15 times more expenditures in child nutrition when income is earned by the father than when it is earned by the mother [Engle, forthcoming]. Similar results have been reported for Chile and Jamaica [Buvinić et al., 1992; Louat et al., 1992], Kenya and Malawi [Kennedy, 1992]. The preference that women have to invest in child well-being appears in poorer families rather than in better-off ones either because investments in children yield greater returns at lower levels of income or because there are fewer competing alternative investments than in higher income households [Kennedy, 1992]. These gender differences in expenditure patterns within households and families suggest that the income that poor women earn can yield higher health or social benefits than the income men earn [World Bank, 1993].

But there are also reports of negative effects of female headship on child well-being. For instance, Wood [1989] found that the survival probability of children in female-headed households in Brazil was significantly lower than those of children in male-headed households. Similar findings have been reported for Zambia and the Philippines [Kumar, 1991; García, 1991]. A likely hypothesis to reconcile positive and negative findings is that women need a minimum level of earnings or income to act on their preferences to invest scarce resources in child well-being. Below a minimum threshold, the economic deprivation which poor women who work in the market suffer is readily (or more easily) transmitted to the next generation.

The consequences of poverty for women's lives and life opportunities are without a doubt substantial but have been much less explored than the consequences of women's poverty on children's well-being. A retrospective study of unpartnered adolescent mothers and their children in Santiago, Chile, indicated that poverty influenced these mothers' marital options. Unmarried mothers coming from better-off families were one-and-a-half times more likely than the poorer women in the study to find a husband and, therefore, to exercise an option that would allow these women to rise above poverty and social disadvantage [Buvinić et al., 1992]. In the case of the poor mothers in this study, there was an adverse selection process in operation (that is, women with a risk of poverty were also women with a risk of lone motherhood), which suggests that policies need to differentiate between socio-economic groups to address the problems of unmarried mothers and children who live in poverty.

VIII. Research and policy implications

The findings reviewed underline the desirability of implementing policies and projects that reinforce the virtuous cycle between women's and children's well-being that can occur in poor families when women have more income and/or control of income, and avoiding those policies that can instead trigger a vicious cycle of deprivation between mothers and children. Social and economic factors that increase poor women's work and economic responsibilities can foster the perpetuation of poverty between mothers and children. These factors include changes in fathers' traditional responsibilities towards children and the effects of declining household incomes during economic downturns. Also included are the unintended consequences of social and economic policy — such as the effects of the promotion of tradables in African agriculture, the decrease in service provision by the state that accompanies SAPs, and welfare-oriented and child-centred interventions that rely heavily on women's unpaid time for their successful implementation. The implementation of these actions without complementary policies that "protect" poor women in their multiple roles as economic producers and reproducers are likely to set in motion or reinforce the vicious cycle of poverty between mothers and children. On the other hand, this vicious cycle can be turned into a virtuous one by raising poor women's productivity in home production as well as their productivity and earnings in labour and product markets.

Alternatively, "empowering" women in other ways so that they can have control over family income, or a say about how it is allocated, could also help transform the vicious cycle of poverty into a virtuous one. Formal schooling strengthens women's autonomy but the returns are delayed and probably overemphasized in the literature. The mobilization of women into women's groups and collectives can be a powerful complementary measure and may "empower" women, but it does not address the central issue of women's work. The most straightforward vehicle to "empower" poor women is to increase their productivity in home and agricultural production, their employment options and the income they obtain from work.

Measures that achieve the above objectives address the *strategic needs* of poor women [Molyneaux, 1985; Moser, 1989]. In most instances, these measures should respond to the unique conditions of women in poverty. Because the circumstances of poor women are sufficiently different from those of better-off women and poor men, interventions that seek to redress gender inequalities (i.e. legal reforms) need complementary measures to effectively reach poor women (i.e. legal aid so that poor women can benefit from these reforms), and universal policies that include elements of self-targeting by the poor need to include specific features to attract women.

Social assistance, welfare and child-centred interventions that meet women's and children's basic needs address the *practical needs* of poor women but do not break the cycle of poverty and deprivation between mothers and children and are, therefore, not effective anti-poverty strategies. Especially ineffective among these can be interventions on behalf of children, communities or women themselves that rely heavily on women's time for their successful implementation, increasing women's time burdens in unpaid activities. Also ineffective are measures that provide women with paid work but at very low or substandard wages. Some compensatory public works programmes in the 1980s, like the *Programa de Apoio al Ingreso Temporal* (PAIT) in Peru, that offered women paid work at a reduction in the hours worked in the marketplace, were probably effective anti-poverty strategies. Others, however, such as the *Programa de Empleo Minimo* (PEM) in Chile, paid very substandard wages to women, and may have reinforced the cycle of poverty between mothers and children.

The short-lived PAIT had a number of features that made it an attractive work option for poor women. It did not require prior training, allowed for flexible work hours, recruited workers from nearby neighbour-hoods so that there were no or very low transportation costs, and allowed women to bring their children to work. It also enabled poor women to substitute paid work for unpaid community participation [Vigier, 1986]. Women's participation in the Maharashtra Employment Guarantee Scheme in India is linked to sites that share the characteristics of the Peruvian PAIT. The PAIT had an explicit policy to reach women, while the majority of the employment promotion programmes for the poor (including the Chilean PEM) instead target poor men, explicitly or implicitly. Included among the latter are the old, but persistent, practice of providing agricultural extension to male farmers and nutrition education to female farmers and the new practice of providing employment to men and social assistance to women as part of "demand-driven" social investment funds. Social investment funds often do not reach women with employment-oriented interventions in part because they have no explicit gender policy and because they depend on the capacity to reach the poor of executing agencies, which are much better equipped to meet women's practical than strategic needs.

In addition to these policy and institutional obstacles, measures that entail increasing poor women's paid work opportunities and income are not popular politically because they both target a powerless constituency and elicit unfounded but pervasive fears of a negative impact of women's new-found economic independence on their traditional family roles. The brief, two-year existence of the PAIT in Peru illustrates the lack of popular support for programmes that transfer income to poor women.

Therefore, critical elements in the design of programmes to address strategic gender needs effectively are explicit gender objectives and a policy to achieve these objectives; gender-disaggregated statistics to monitor programme implementation and measure impact; executing agencies which can attract and work with women participants; and budget allocations to strengthen the capacity of institutions to implement and monitor gender-responsive productivity-enhancing and employment pro-grammes for the poor. Governments and donors need to invest in the growth of women-based NGOs that can work with women among the poor.

The reach of interventions that address women's strategic needs is restricted, however. Their impact is often short-lived and, while they can help to contain the cycle of poverty between mothers and children, they cannot in themselves transform women's economic activities. Changes in the policy environment are required to accomplish the latter. These include agricultural policies that target poor farmers and give women farmers access to land titles; financial policies that promote the growth of small enterprises and foster entrepreneurship among women; and labour-intensive "pro-poor" economic growth policies. In addition, governments need to invest in upgrading women's skills in traditional as well as non-traditional occupations that can compete in national as well as export markets; and in a series of complementary measures, including overhauling social security systems, establishing gender-friendly regulatory frameworks for agri-cultural and industrial growth, and legislating on child-care options.

Research needs to separate households from families and seek to understand the formation, structure and dynamics of families maintained by women. Studies need to obtain more reliable measures of women's wealth and well-being and investigate the determinants of women's poverty. Longitudinal prospective and retrospective studies are required to provide a narrative for events in women's lives, assess the transmission of disadvantage between mothers and children, and disentangle cause-effect relationships in the determinants and consequences of women's poverty. Trend analyses are required to track changes in women's workloads and work participation as a result of changes in economic conditions and in the implementation of economic and social policies. Impact studies of the effects of economic and social reforms on the situation of women in poverty are urgently required, as are thoughtful analyses of the mechanics, costs and consequences of targeting interventions to poor women and to woman-maintained families. The policy-oriented research agenda is perhaps equally as ambitious as the policy agenda and both require financial resources. Investing in women in poverty should, however, be an effective use of scarce development resources.

Bibliographical references

Acosta, F. Forthcoming. "Análisis demográfico de la jefatura de hogar femenina en México", paper prepared for joint ICRW/Population Council Series on Family Structure, Female Headship and Maintenance of Families, and Poverty.

Barros, R. Paes de, et al. 1989. "Female headed households, poverty, and the welfare of children in Brazil", paper prepared for the World Bank.

Bruce, J.; Lloyd, C. Forthcoming. "Beyond female headship: Family research and policy issues for the 1990s", in Haddad, L. et al. (eds.): *Intrahoushold resource allocation: policy issues and research methods*. Baltimore, MD: Johns Hopkins University Press.

Buvinić, M. et al. 1989. "The impact of a credit project for women and men microentrepreneurs in Quito, Ecuador", in *Women's ventures: Assistance to the informal sector in Latin America*. West Hartford, Connecticut, Kumarian Press.

Buvinić, M.; Valenzuela, J. P.; Molina, T.; González, E. 1992. "The fortunes of adolescent mothers and their children: A case study on the transmission of poverty in Santiago, Chile", in *Population and Development Review* (New York), 18(2).

Buvinić, M.; Valenzuela, J. P. Forthcoming. "The intergenerational transmission of poverty in Santiago, Chile", in Haddad, L. et al. (eds.), op. cit.

Casanovas, R. et al. 1985. "Los trabajadores por cuenta propia en el mercado de trabajo: El caso de la cuidad de La Paz", in *El sector informal urbano en los paises andinos*. Quito and Guayaquil, Ecuador, ILDIS y CEPESIU.

Chipande, G. H. R. 1987. "Innovation adoption among female-headed households: The case of Malawi", in *Development and Change* (London), 18, pp. 315-327.

Commonwealth Secretariat. 1991. *Women and structural adjustment: Selected case studies commissioned for a Commonwealth group of experts*. Commonwealth Economic Papers No. 22. London, the Commonwealth Secretariat.

Engle, P. Forthcoming. "Influences of mother's and father's income on children's nutritional status in Guatemala", in *Social Science and Medicine* (Oxford).

Folbre, N. 1991. *Mothers on their own: Policy issues for developing countries*. Paper prepared for the joint ICRW/Population Council series on "The determinants and consequences of female-headed households".

Francke, M. 1992. *Women and the labor market in Lima, Peru: Weathering economic crises*. Paper prepared for the ICRW Seminar on "Weathering economic crises: Women's responses to recession in Latin America, 11 August. Washington, DC.

Fürstenberg, F.; Brooks-Gunn, S.; Morgan, P. 1987. *Adolescent mothers in later life.* Cambridge, Massachusetts, Cambridge University Press.

Garfinkel, I.; McLanahan, S. S. 1986. *Single mothers and their children.* Washington, DC, The Urban Institute Press.

Haddad, L. et al. (eds.). Forthcoming. *Intrahousehold resource allocation: Policy issues and research methods.* Baltimore, MD, Johns Hopkins University Press.

Humphries, J. 1988. "Women and work", in Eatwell, J. et al. (eds.): *The New Palgrave: A Dictionary of Economics.* New York, Stockton Press.

ICRW (International Center for Research on Women). 1992. *Weathering economic crises: women's responses to the recession in Latin America and the Caribbean. Selected country studies.* Washington, DC, ICRW.

Jazairy, I.; Alamgir, M.; Panuccio, T. 1992. *The state of world rural poverty: An inquiry into its causes and consequences.* New York, New York University Press.

Kennedy, E. 1992. *Effects of gender of head of household on women's and children's nutritional status.* Paper presented at the workshop on "The effects of policies and programs on women", 16 January, Washington, DC.

King, E.; Evenson R. E. 1983. "Time allocation and home production in Philippine rural households", in Buvinić, M. (eds.): *Women and poverty in the Third World.* Baltimore, MD, Johns Hopkins University Press.

Koussoudji, S.; Mueller, E. 1983. "The economic and demographic status of female-headed households in rural Botswana", in *Economic Development and Cultural Change* (Chicago), Vol. 21, July, pp. 831-859.

Kumar, S. K. 1991. *Income sources of the malnourished poor in rural Zambia.* Working paper. Washington, DC, International Food Policy Research Institute.

Leslie, J. 1988. "Women's work and child nutrition in the Third World", in *World Development* (New York), 16(11), pp. 1341-1362.

—. Lycette, M.; Buvinić, M. 1988. "Weathering economic crises: The crucial role of women in health", in Bell, D. E.; Reich, M. R. (eds.): *Health, nutrition and economic crises.* Dover, MA, Auburn House Publishing Company.

Lloyd, C. B.; Brandon, A. J. 1991. *Women's roles in maintaining households: Poverty and gender inequality in Ghana.* Prepared for ICRW/Population Council joint project on "Family structure, female headship and poverty in developing countries".

Louat, F. M.; Grosh, E.; Gaag, J. van der. 1992. *Welfare implications of female-headship in Jamaican households.* Paper presented at the International Food Policy Research Institute Workshop on "Intrahousehold resource allocation: policy issues and research methods," Washington, DC, 12-14 February.

McLeod, R. 1988. *Shelter experiences of female heads of households in Kingston, Jamaica.* United Nations Center for Human Settlements (HABITAT). Draft presented at a joint ICRW/Population Council Seminar II on "Consequences of female headship and female maintenance", Washington, DC, 27-28 February 1989.

Merrick, T. W.; Schmink, M. 1983. "Households headed by women and urban poverty in Brazil", in Buvinić, M. (eds.): *Women and poverty in the Third World.* Baltimore, MD, The Johns Hopkins University Press.

Mitra, A. 1981. "Participation of women in socio-economic development", in *Women and Development* (Paris, UNESCO).

Molyneux, M. 1985. "Mobilization without emancipation? Women's interests, State and revolution in Nicaragua", in *Feminist Studies,* 11(2).

Moser, C. O. N. 1993. "Adjustment from below: Low-income women, time and the triple role in Guayquil, Ecuador", in Radcliffe, S. A; Westwood, S. (eds.): *Viva: Women and popular protest in Latin America.* London, Routledge.

—. 1989. "Gender planning in the Third World: Meeting practical and strategic gender needs", in *World Development* (New York), 17(11), pp. 1799-1825.

—. Herbert, A. J.; Makonnen, R. E. 1993. *Urban poverty in the context of structural adjustment, recent evidence and policy responses.* Transportation, Water and Urban Development Department Discussion Paper No. 4. Washington, DC, World Bank.

OECD (Organisation for Economic Cooperation and Development). 1976. *The 1974-1975 recession and the employment of women.* Paris, OECD.

Palmer, I. 1991. *Gender and population in the adjustment of african economies: Planning for change.* Geneva, International Labour Office.

Popkin, B. M. 1983. "Rural women, work, and child welfare in the Philippines", in Buvinić, M. et al. (eds.): *Women and poverty in the Third World.* Baltimore, MD, Johns Hopkins University Press.

PREALC (Programa Regional del Empleo para América Latina y el Caribe). 1981. *Sector informal: Funcionamiento y políticas.* Santiago, PREALC-ILO.

PRB (Population Reference Bureau). 1992. *Chartbook: Africa demographic and health surveys.* Washington, DC, Population Reference Bureau.

Psacharopoulos, G.; Tzannatos, Z. 1992. *Women's employment and pay in Latin America: Overview and methodology.* World Bank Regional and Sectoral Studies. Washington, DC, The World Bank.

Rogers, B. 1991. *Female headship in the Dominican Republic: Alternative definitions and implications for food consumption and nutrition.* Medford, Tufts University School of Nutrition.

Rosales, O. V. 1979. *La mujer chilena en la fuerza de trabajo: participación, empleo, y desempleo (1957-1977).* Santiago, Chile, Universidad de Chile.

—. 1979. *La mujer chilena en la fuerza de trabajo: Participación, empleo y desempleo (1957-1977).* Santiago, Chile, University of Chile.

Ross, H.; Sawhill, I. 1976. *Families in transition: The growth of households headed by women*. Washington, DC, The Urban Institute.

Singh, S.; Wulf, D. 1990. *Today's adolescents, tomorrow's parents: A portrait of the Americas*. New York, The Alan Guttmacher Institute.

Standing, G. 1989. "Global feminization through flexible labor", in *World Development* (New York), 17(7), pp. 1077-1095.

Thomas, D. 1990. "Intra-household resource allocation: An inferential approach", in *Journal of Human Resources* (Madison, Wisconsin), XXV(4), pp. 635-664.

United Nations. 1984. *La mujer en el sector popular urbano: América Latina y el Caribe*

United Nations. 1991. *The world's women: Trends and statistics 1970-1990*, New York,. Santiago de Chile, United Nations, p. 246.

Vigier, M. E. 1986. *El impacto del pait en el empleo y los ingresos: Lima metropolitana 1986*. Lima, Proyecto Planificación del Mercado Laboral, OIT.

Visaria, P.; Visaria, L. 1985. "Indian households with female heads: Their incidence, characteristics and level of living", in Jain, D.; Banerjee, N. (eds.): *Tyranny of the household*. New Delhi, Shakti Books.

—. 1980. "Poverty and living standards in Asia", in *Population and Development Review* (New York), 6(2), pp. 189-223.

Wood, C. H. 1989. *Women-headed households and child mortality in Brazil, 1960-1980*. Draft presented at joint ICRW/Population Council Seminar II on "Consequences of female headship and female maintenance". Washington, DC, 27-28 February.

World Bank. 1993. *World Development Report 1993: Investing in health*. Washington, DC, The World Bank.

—. 1990. *World Development Report 1990: Poverty*. Washington, DC, The World Bank.